T0316590

Cambridge Elements

Elements of Paleontology
edited by
Colin D. Sumrall
University of Tennessee

NICHE EVOLUTION AND PHYLOGENETIC COMMUNITY PALEOECOLOGY OF LATE ORDOVICIAN CRINOIDS

Selina R. Cole

National Museum of Natural History, Smithsonian Institution and American Museum of Natural History

David F. Wright

National Museum of Natural History, Smithsonian Institution and American Museum of Natural History

CAMBRIDGE
UNIVERSITY PRESS

University Printing House, Cambridge CB2 8BS, United Kingdom

One Liberty Plaza, 20th Floor, New York, NY 10006, USA

477 Williamstown Road, Port Melbourne, VIC 3207, Australia

314–321, 3rd Floor, Plot 3, Splendor Forum, Jasola District Centre, New Delhi – 110025, India

103 Penang Road, #05–06/07, Visioncrest Commercial, Singapore 238467

Cambridge University Press is part of the University of Cambridge.

It furthers the University's mission by disseminating knowledge in the pursuit of education, learning, and research at the highest international levels of excellence.

www.cambridge.org
Information on this title: www.cambridge.org/9781108810012
DOI: 10.1017/9781108893459

© Selina R. Cole and David F. Wright 2022

First published 2022

A catalogue record for this publication is available from the British Library.

ISBN 978-1-108-81001-2 Paperback
ISSN 2517-780X (online)
ISSN 2517-7796 (print)

Additional resources for this publication at www.cambridge.org/colewright

Niche Evolution and Phylogenetic Community Paleoecology of Late Ordovician Crinoids

Elements of Paleontology

DOI: 10.1017/9781108893459
First published online: April 2022

Selina R. Cole
National Museum of Natural History, Smithsonian Institution and American Museum of Natural History

David F. Wright
National Museum of Natural History, Smithsonian Institution and American Museum of Natural History

Author for correspondence: Selina R. Cole, colesr@si.edu

Abstract: Fossil crinoids are exceptionally suited to deep-time studies of community paleoecology and niche partitioning. By merging ecomorphological traits and phylogenetic data, this Element summarizes niche occupation and community paleoecology of crinoids from the Bromide fauna of Oklahoma (Sandbian, Upper Ordovician). Patterns of community structure and niche evolution are evaluated over a ~5-million-year period through comparison with the Brechin Lagerstätte (Katian, Upper Ordovician). Filtration fan density, food size selectivity, and body size are established as major axes defining niche differentiation, and niche occupation is strongly controlled by phylogeny. Ecological strategies were relatively static over the study interval at high taxonomic scales, but niche differentiation and specialization increased in most subclades. Changes in disparity and species richness indicate that the transition between the early-middle Paleozoic Crinoid Evolutionary Faunas was already underway by the Katian due to ecological drivers and was not triggered by the Late Ordovician mass extinction.

Keywords: phylogenetic comparative methods, Crinoidea, disparity, niche differentiation, functional ecology

ISBNs: 9781108810012 (PB), 9781108893459 (OC)
ISSNs: 2517-780X (online), 2517-7796 (print)

Contents

1 Introduction

Ecological communities have changed dramatically over the course of geological history as a result of environmental change, biotic interactions, evolution of new higher taxa, and extinction (Vermeij, 1987; Kelley et al., 2003; Bush & Bambach, 2011; Lyons et al. 2019). At the ecosystem scale, a variety of approaches have been used to evaluate broad patterns of resource utilization, functional diversity, and complexity through deep time using theoretical concepts and methodological approaches like tiering, ecospace filling, limiting components, ecosystem engineering, ecological clustering, network analysis, niche modeling, and abundance distributions (e.g., Ausich, 1983; Bambach, 1983; Ausich & Bottjer, 1982; Wagner et al., 2006; Bambach et al., 2007; Novack-Gottshall, 2007; Erwin, 2008; Stigall, 2012; Dineen et al., 2014; Muscente et al., 2018; Novack-Gottshall et al., 2022). Many of these methods have also been successfully applied to community-level investigations to evaluate various aspects of ecology or make comparisons between paleocommunities (e.g., Brame & Stigall, 2014; Darroch et al., 2018; Perera and Stigall, 2018; Whittle et al., 2019; Cole et al., 2020; Nanglu et al., 2020). However, other ecological aspects of paleocommunities relating to niche partitioning, assembly, and structure are not readily captured by these methods and have received far less attention in past studies, particularly for clades of fossil marine invertebrates.

Niches are complex and multidimensional, reflecting a wide range of traits, behaviors, and abiotic factors that dictate the functional position of organisms within their environment, biotic interactions, and resource partitioning within communities (Hutchinson, 1978). Because of their fundamental role in ecology, niches are a necessary component for fully understanding community structure and evolution through deep time. Characterizing species niches is challenging in the fossil record, in part because of difficulties in extracting relevant biological/ ecological information from fossils. As a result, many studies have focused on characterizing niches using abiotic data that can be extracted from the rocks associated with specimen occurrences, such as water depth, substrate consistency, turbidity, and temperature (e.g., Meyer et al., 2002; Holland & Zaffos, 2011; Stigall, 2012; Myers et al., 2015; Antell et al., 2021). Others have used one or more ecologically significant traits like body size as proxies for niche partitioning at broad levels, especially for groups like vertebrates where relationships between size and other niche parameters are well understood (e.g., Andrews et al., 1979; Pineda-Munoz et al., 2016; Fraser & Lyons, 2020; Schroeder et al., 2021). Within marine invertebrate faunas, classic work by Bambach (1983) identified three major categories – feeding, motility, and tiering – that could be used to characterize ecospace utilization, and subsequent investigations have expanded upon this approach to encompass additional ecological components and methods (Novack-Gottshall, 2007, 2016a, 2016b; Villéger et al., 2011). Although these categorical elements have been used to describe functional diversity within groups (e.g., Schumm et al., 2019; Novack-Gottshall et al., 2022), they are typically too broad to capture the range of variation between ecologically similar species and thus do not represent niche concepts at the species level (Bambach et al., 2007; see Hadly et al., 2009). As a result, ecospace approaches have generally focused on patterns of functional diversity of whole ecosystems rather than the structure and dynamics of species niches within communities.

Some fossil organisms readily preserve anatomical features that can be linked back to ecological functions, referred to as ecomorphological traits. When multiple ecomorphological traits are identifiable for a study group, they can be used in multivariate analyses to evaluate the relative position of species in ecomorphospace. They can also function as a proxy for niche occupation if traits are thought to capture major components of niche differentiation (Ricklefs & Miles, 1994; Pianka et al., 2017). Analyses of ecomorphospace occupation have been conducted widely across fossil and living taxa as a means of quantifying ecological variation, typically with continuous and/or discrete characters, and either with or without direct inferences of niche occupation being made (e.g., Van Valkenburg, 1994; Weiser et al., 2006; Anderson, 2009; Fischer et al., 2017; Pianka, 2017; Walton & Korn, 2018; Cole et al., 2019; Mallon, 2019; Cole & Hopkins, 2021). Using ecomorphospace to characterize species niches in multidimensional trait space is a powerful approach for community-level studies because it operationalizes complex concepts like niche breadth and permits investigation of a wide range of hypotheses relating to community assembly, biotic interactions, and resource partitioning. This approach is not without its challenges, however, especially when it comes to identifying ecomorphological traits in the fossil record. In both living and fossil organisms, ecomorphological traits typically relate back to aspects of feeding, mobility, behavior, biotic interactions, environmental interactions (e.g., interface with water currents or substrate), life history, and/or tolerance of abiotic conditions – in short, any traits that affect an organism's ecological niche (Wainwright, 1991; Winemiller, 1991; Bock, 1994; Van Valkenburgh, 1994; for examples of ecomorphological trait identification across diverse clades, see Zanno & Makovicky, 2011; Fountain-Jones et al., 2014; Pianka et al., 2017; Barr, 2018; Cole et al., 2019). In some fossils, the ecological importance of certain traits may be unambiguous, such as dental morphology in mammals, which relates directly to dietary ecology (Evans & Pineda-Munoz, 2018). However, the ecological relevance of other ecomorphological traits may be less intuitive. For example, detailed hydrodynamic studies have identified certain features that are ecologically important for feeding and stability of both fossil cinctan echinoderms (Rahman et al., 2020) and Ediacaran organisms (Rahman et al. 2015; Gibson et al., 2021). Similarly, the ecological roles of many other traits in fossil organisms have only been confidently identified through a variety of creative approaches, such as biomechanical and other experimental studies (e.g., Kammer 1985; Baumiller & Ausich, 1996; Carrano, 1997; Peterman et al., 2021), evidence of interactions between co-occurring organisms (e.g., Baumiller & Gahn, 2003; Taylor, 2016; Feng et al., 2017), or study of modern analogues (Stanley, 1970; Macurda & Meyer, 1974; Meyer & Ausich, 1983). As a result, extensive expertise in the morphology, taxonomy, biomechanics, biotic interactions, and/or behavior of the study group is often required in order to diagnose a robust suite of ecomorphological traits.

Incorporating phylogenetic perspectives into studies of species niches can provide further insight into community ecology and niche evolution. When integrated with community-level data, phylogenies can be used to recognize evolutionary changes in patterns of assembly, structure, and trait distributions within communities, in addition to the underlying processes responsible for generating observed patterns. Further, combining phylogenies with data on niche occupation can allow identification of phenomena like niche convergence, divergence, and niche conservatism. Although phylogenetic community ecology has been applied widely to studies of modern systems (for reviews see Webb et al., 2002; Cavender-Bares et al., 2009; Qian & Jiang, 2014), it is challenging to obtain both robust phylogenetic hypotheses and detailed ecomorphological data for many fossil taxa. Nevertheless, the merging of phylogenetic and paleoecological perspectives represents a promising area of paleontological research (Lamsdell et al., 2017; Cole et al., 2019), and case studies using these approaches are becoming increasingly widespread, especially for terrestrial vertebrate communities (Raia, 2010; Fraser et al., 2015; Polly et al., 2017, Fraser & Lyons, 2017, 2020). Although these methods have been less commonly applied to invertebrate fossil groups (e.g., Cole et al., 2019; Chang & Skipwith, 2020), fossil crinoids are a particularly promising system because they preserve extensive ecological data and have a robust phylogenetic framework (Wright et al., 2017; Cole et al., 2019). As a result, they are the only fossil invertebrate group for which community-level niche dynamics have been studied in a phylogenetic context (Cole et al., 2019; Cole et al., 2020) and have the potential to provide deep-time perspectives on niche evolution, niche dynamics, and community ecology.

1.1 Crinoid Paleoecology and Niche Partitioning

Among fossil marine invertebrates, it is often challenging to identify characters with unambiguous ecological functions, which can hinder quantitative investigations of niche evolution in deep time. Crinoids are ideally suited for questions that require knowledge of species ecology in deep time, because their skeletons preserve many features that directly correspond to ecological functions. This allows fossil crinoid niches to be quantitatively reconstructed with a high degree of fidelity. Notably, the ecology of both fossil and living crinoids has been studied extensively and cross-compared (Meyer, 1973, 1979; Macurda & Meyer, 1974; Ausich, 1980; Ausich & Bottjer, 1982; Baumiller, 1997; Brower, 2007, 2013; Kitazawa et al., 2007; Meyer et al., 2021; Messing et al, 2017). As passive suspension feeders, crinoids primarily partition niches through differences in feeding ecology, such as the differentiation of feeding structures (for example, the number, arrangement, and structure of arms and pinnules [Meyer, 1979; Ausich, 1980; Kitazawa et al., 2007]) and tiering (the height of the crinoid crown and feeding apparatus above the substrate, most commonly controlled by stem length [Ausich & Bottjer, 1982]). The role these traits play in crinoid feeding ecology and niche partitioning has been extensively reviewed elsewhere (e.g., Baumiller, 2008; Cole et al., 2019: Figure 1).

Recent work established a series of continuous ecomorphological traits that could be used to capture niche differentiation in crinoids through variation in feeding structures and body size (Cole, 2017a, 2019). In a subsequent study,

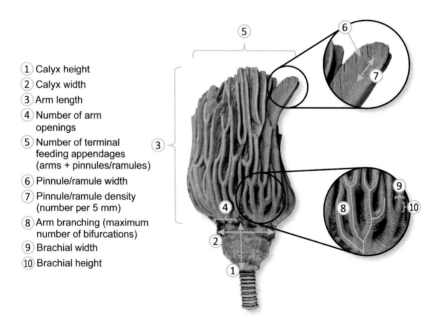

1. Calyx height
2. Calyx width
3. Arm length
4. Number of arm openings
5. Number of terminal feeding appendages (arms + pinnules/ramules)
6. Pinnule/ramule width
7. Pinnule/ramule density (number per 5 mm)
8. Arm branching (maximum number of bifurcations)
9. Brachial width
10. Brachial height

Figure 1 Collected measurements of ecomorphologic traits. Representative specimen shown is *Actinocrinites gibsoni* (Mississippian, Cincinnati Museum Center, CMCIP 71449; photo courtesy of W. I. Ausich).

ecomorphological traits were combined with phylogenetic data to investigate niche occupation and community paleoecology of crinoids from the Upper Ordovician (Katian) Brechin Lagerstätte and to test a wide range of hypotheses relating to community structure, niche partitioning, and niche conservatism within the fauna (Cole et al., 2019). Although this investigation primarily focused on a single fauna, it also looked at differences in filtration fan density between crinoids from the Ordovician-age Brechin Lagerstätte and the Mississippian-age Edwardsville Fauna and found that substantial shifts occurred through time, especially within subclass Pentacrinoidea (Cole et al., 2019). Notably, this study also provided a methodological proof of concept for phylogenetic investigations into the long-term evolution of crinoid niches and the structure of ecological communities through deep time.

In this Element, we apply a series of trait- and phylogeny-based analyses to crinoids from the Upper Ordovician (Sandbian) Bromide Formation of Oklahoma in order to characterize patterns of community assembly and niche space occupation. In addition, we compare the paleoecology of crinoids from the Bromide fauna to that of crinoids from the geologically younger Brechin Lagerstätte (Upper Ordovician, Katian), which was investigated in a previous study (Cole et al., 2019). We further characterize and compare aspects of crinoid functional ecology between the two faunas via application of disparity analyses to community-wide ecomorphological trait data. Through these comparisons, we evaluate niche partitioning, niche evolution, phylogenetic structure of niches, and changes in community structure over a ~5 million-year period. This work highlights the utility of integrating phylogenetic and trait-based methods for application to paleocommunities and provides a robust framework for future investigations of crinoid community evolution and changes in niche space through time.

2 Characteristics of the Bromide and Brechin Crinoid Faunas

The Upper Ordovician was a key interval in the early evolutionary history of crinoids. The earliest known crinoids are from the Lower Ordovician (Tremadocian) of Utah (Guensburg & Sprinkle, 2003), but crinoid taxonomic diversity remained relatively low until the Middle Ordovician (Peters & Ausich, 2008). During the Middle–Late Ordovician, rapid diversification of crinoids occurred as part of the Great Ordovician Biodiversification of marine invertebrate life (Webby et al., 2004; Wright & Toom, 2017). Peak genus-level diversity was reached during the Katian stage of the Upper Ordovician before it dropped precipitously during the Late Ordovician mass extinction across the Katian–Hirnantian boundary (Peters & Ausich, 2008; Wright & Toom, 2017; Cole, 2018). In crinoids, this rapid diversification occurred at both the genus and species levels and led to greater morphological and ecological variation (Foote, 1994, 1999; Deline & Ausich, 2011; Wright, 2017a; Deline et al., 2018, 2020; Cole & Hopkins, 2021) and increases in community complexity (Cole et al., 2020) during the Upper Ordovician. As a result, the Upper Ordovician is a dynamic interval of time in crinoid evolutionary history that is ideal for evaluating the evolution of niche occupation and community assembly in early crinoid communities. In terms of taxonomic richness, the two faunas compared here – the Bromide and the Brechin – have the highest known crinoid diversities from the Sandbian and Katian, respectively. As a result, both paleocommunities should be broadly representative of Laurentian crinoid faunas during these stages of the Upper Ordovician. For example, the relative proportions of major groups that make up the Brechin fauna are comparable to those of other Katian-age crinoid assemblages (Cole et al., 2017; Cole et al., 2020).

When making comparisons between fossil communities, it is important to account for potential biases that could generate spurious results, such as those relating to differences in taphonomy, depositional environment, and sampling intensity. The following sections summarize these aspects of the Bromide and Brechin crinoid faunas to highlight both strengths and limitations of the comparative study of these two crinoid paleocommunities.

2.1 Taxonomic Diversity

The Bromide Formation is the most diverse echinoderm fauna known throughout the entire fossil record from a single formation and is the most species-rich assemblage of Ordovician crinoids. As of 1982, more than 11,000 echinoderm specimens had been recovered from the Bromide Formation, representing more than 60 genera across 13 classes (Sprinkle, 1982a). Echinoderms from the Bromide fauna, including a diverse crinoid assemblage, were described in detail in a 1982 monograph (Sprinkle, 1982a) that remains the most comprehensive treatment of Bromide echinoderms to date. Including subsequent studies describing new taxa, crinoid diversity from the Bromide Formation currently stands at 28 genera and 38 valid named species. However, specimens representing at least nine additional taxa have been figured in published literature but left indeterminate or questionably assigned because of poor preservation (e.g., Sprinkle 1982a), and other specimens representing new species or higher taxa are still awaiting formal description (e.g., Sprinkle et al., 2015, 2018). As a result, the total diversity of crinoids from the Bromide Formation is likely closer to 50 species.

The Brechin Lagerstätte is the second most diverse Ordovician crinoid fauna known. A description of the Brechin fauna, historically referred to as the "Kirkfield," was first published by Frank Springer in 1911, but the faunal list was incomplete. Subsequent collecting produced a large number of exceptionally preserved specimens that were used as the basis for a reevaluation of the diversity of the fauna. These revisions of the fauna were covered in a series of recent publications that resulted in the recognition and description of 15 new species and three new genera, bringing the known diversity of Brechin crinoids to 27 genera and 39 nominal species (Cole et al., 2018, 2020; Ausich et al., 2018; Wright et al., 2019). Similar to the Bromide fauna, the Brechin also preserves a number of species belonging to other echinoderm classes (e.g., Sumrall & Gahn, 2006; Blake & Koniecki 2019, 2020), although most have not received comprehensive taxonomic assessment. In addition to echinoderms, both the Brechin and the Bromide preserve abundant faunas that are typical constituents of benthic Ordovician communities, such as trilobites, bryozoans, and brachiopods (Brett & Liddell, 1978).

2.2 Geology and Paleoenvironmental Setting

The Bromide Formation extends throughout a large portion of the Arbuckle Mountains and Criner Hills regions of south-central Oklahoma. Although the Bromide is over 100 m thick, echinoderm fossils have primarily been recovered from two zones in the middle Mountain Lake Member and a cluster of horizons in the overlying Pooleville Member. These fossil-bearing horizons are distributed over a ~75 m section of the Bromide Formation, and crinoids have been collected from numerous localities for each of these zones (Sprinkle, 1982b). Similar to the crinoid occurrences in the Brechin fauna (the Bobcaygeon and Verulam formations; see the discussion in the following paragraph), crinoid-bearing horizons in the Bromide Formation are predominantly shale beds interbedded with grainstones, packstones, and wackestones (Sprinkle, 1982b; Carlucci et al., 2014). During the interval of interest for this Element, deposition of the Bromide Formation occurred along a carbonate-dominant ramp in a NW-SE trending trough (Carlucci et al., 2014). The fossiliferous horizons from which crinoids have been recovered are interpreted to have been deposited in shallow-to deep-shelf paleoenvironments (Longman, 1982; Carlucci et al., 2014). The Bromide Formation is thought to span the majority of the Sandbian stage (Carlucci et al., 2014), which is approximately 5.4 myr in length, concluding around 453 Ma (Goldman et al., 2020). However, fossil crinoids do not occur in the lower sandstone member (Sprinkle, 1982b), so the total age range spanned by crinoids from the Bromide is much shorter.

Crinoids from the Brechin Lagerstätte have been recovered from multiple quarries in the Lake Simcoe region of southern Ontario, Canada (Cole et al., 2018). These quarries are all located within ~6 km of the town of Brechin, Ontario, for which the fauna is named. Crinoid-bearing horizons are present throughout a ~20 m thick interval that spans the uppermost ~15 m of the Bobcaygeon Formation and ~5 m of the lowermost Verulam Formation (for further discussions of stratigraphic divisions, correlations, and nomenclature for the Upper Ordovician of southern Ontario, see Armstrong [2000], Cole et al. [2018], and Paton & Brett [2019]). The Bobcaygeon and overlying Verulam formations are composed of bioclastic grainstones, packstones, and wackestones that are interbedded with calcareous shales and siltstones. These strata are interpreted to have been deposited in a proximal carbonate shelf environment that varied in depth from shallow shelf in the Bobcaygeon to deep shelf in the Verulam (Armstrong, 2000), with gradual deepening moving upward through the Bobcaygeon to Verulam (Liberty, 1969). Fossil horizons that make up the Brechin Lagerstätte span the lower portion of the Katian within the middle-upper Bobcaygeon and lower Verulam Formations. Although numerical ages for this interval are not tightly constrained, the Verulam–Bobcaygeon boundary should be approximately 451 Ma and the fauna should span an interval of roughly 2 million years or less (Sproat et al., 2015; Paton & Brett, 2019; Goldman et al., 2020). Thus, the estimated time between the latest fossiliferous horizons of the Bromide and the earliest fossiliferous horizons comprising the Brechin fauna is relatively short (~2 myr), and the time elapsed between median ages for the faunas is <5 million years.

2.3 Taphonomy and "Paleocommunities"

The Bromide and Brechin faunas are similar taphonomically, although there is greater taphonomic heterogeneity between fossil-bearing horizons in the Bromide Formation. A greater proportion of articulated cups and crowns are recovered from the Brechin than from the Bromide, but the sheer number of specimens recovered from the Bromide has resulted in a large sample of well-preserved specimens with arms intact. As a result, the two faunas are broadly comparable in terms of taphonomy and specimen-level sampling intensity of their constituent species.

Because crinoids disarticulate rapidly upon death, preservation of specimens with arms and/or stems intact signals rapid burial and little to no time-averaging or transport (Donovan, 1991; Brett et al., 1997; Ausich, 2001, 2021; Ausich & Baumiller, 1993). As a result, horizons of well-preserved crinoids, such as those recovered from the Bromide and Brechin faunas, should not be subject to spatial or temporal averaging (Kidwell & Behrensmeyer, 1993). Individual horizons of well-preserved crinoids can be treated as ecological snapshots (Ausich, 2016), and this approach has been applied to hardground surfaces in the Brechin fauna (Taylor & Brett, 1996; Paton et al., 2019). However, here we combine all crinoid-bearing horizons from the Bromide and Brechin faunas in order to provide reasonable sample sizes. As a result, as they have been assembled here, the Bromide and Brechin datasets do not represent ecological snapshots per se. Instead, they reflect recurring species assemblages that are both temporally and spatially restricted (e.g., within a single basin), which is consistent with the traditional use of the term "paleocommunity" in paleoecological literature (e.g., Walker and Laporte, 1970; Ausich, 1980; Bennington & Bambach, 1996; Wagner et al., 2006; Perera & Stigall, 2018; Lyons et al., 2019).

3 Methods

3.1 Collection and Vetting of Ecomorphologic Trait Data

We use the term "ecomorphologic traits" to describe morphological characters that directly correspond to or strongly correlate with ecological functions. Following the model of crinoid niche differentiation outlined by Ausich (1980), Cole (2017a), and later expanded upon by Cole et al. (2019), we collected data for ten ecomorphological traits and calculated an additional three composite characters (Figure 1). Measured characters include (1) calyx height, (2) calyx width, (3) arm length, (4) number of arm openings, (5) arm branching, quantified as the maximum number of in-line bifurcations, (6) number of terminal feeding appendages (Ω), (7) brachial width, (8) brachial height, measured at the midpoint of the arms, (9) pinnule/ramule density, and (10) pinnule/ramule width. In addition, we calculated three composite characters that represent important aspects of crinoid morphology and ecology: (1) calyx volume (V), calculated using the standard equation for a cone, (2) filtration fan area (f_A), calculated using the Ausich (1980) equation with modifications by Cole (2017a), and (3) filtration fan density (F_D), calculated by dividing the total number of terminal feeding appendages (Ω, quantitative trait 6) by the total area of the filtration fan (f_A). These traits have been identified as having ecological functions based on a large number of previous studies that include investigations of crinoid biomechanics, functional morphology, feeding in modern crinoids, and biotic interactions (e.g., Meyer 1973, 1979; Macurda & Meyer, 1974; Ausich, 1980; Kammer, 1985; Baumiller & Ausich, 1996; Meyer & Ausich, 1996; Baumiller, 1997, 2008; Brower, 2007, 2013; Meyer et al., 2021). More detailed descriptions of crinoid ecology, trait measurements, and calculation of composite characters are given in Cole et al. (2019: Figure 1) and the Supplemental Materials.

We collected ecomorphologic data from 95 specimens representing 37 species from the Bromide fauna. Specimens representing juveniles were not included in the study. *Cleiocrinus ornatus* Kolata 1982 was the only named species from the fauna for which data were not collected because it is known only from fragmentary material where fundamental measurements like calyx height and width could not be collected. Of the 37 species for which data were collected, 36 are currently valid named species, and one is represented by an unidentified specimen belonging to the disparid family Cincinnaticrinidae (Sprinkle, 1982a). This specimen has not been assigned a genus or species name because it does not preserve the posterior interray, which is necessary for classification at finer taxonomic scales. However, it was suitable for inclusion in this Element because it preserves a complete calyx and partial arms and unquestionably represents a unique taxon from the Bromide fauna.

Ecomorphological data were collected from Brechin Lagerstätte crinoids in a previous study by Cole et al. (2019) using the same methods that were here applied to the Bromide fauna. For this Element, we added trait data for three additional Brechin species so that all known taxa were included. These species were *Grenprisia springeri*, based on a new, well-preserved specimen (Wright et al., 2019), *Abludoglyptocirnus steinheimerae*, which was only recently described from the fauna (Cole et al., 2020), and *Cleiocirnus regius*, which did not have any specimens available for study in the original paleoecological investigation. The three composite characters – fan area, fan density, and calyx volume – were also calculated for each species from the Brechin Lagerstätte. In total, the Brechin dataset was compiled from measurements of 168 specimens across all 39 species. For both the Bromide and Brechin datasets, mean values for measured and composite ecomorphological traits were calculated for each species and used for all subsequent analyses.

Some crinoid species from the Bromide and Brechin are known only from poorly preserved specimens and have extensive missing data. In addition, the methods used here would ideally be applicable to crinoid assemblages that are not as well preserved as the Bromide and Brechin, so it is necessary to understand the effect that missing data has on the loss of ecological information. Previous work established the significant effect that taphonomic degradation can have on reconstructing morphological disparity in crinoids and other echinoderms (Deline & Thomka, 2017) based on known patterns of disarticulation at different taphonomic grades (Brett et al., 1997). Here, we conducted a series of sensitivity tests using four different thresholds for missing data to establish a similar understanding of how taphonomic degradation affects the loss of ecological information in crinoids (Supplemental Materials). Based on the results of these sensitivity tests, we determined that only taxa preserving at least partial arms adequately recover patterns of niche occupation, so all remaining analyses were conducted using the vetted datasets that excluded species without at least partial arms preserved (Figure S1; see Supplemental Materials for additional discussion of sensitivity tests). This threshold was chosen because it simultaneously minimizes the amount of missing data and maximizes the number of species that could be reliably included (30 out of 37 Bromide species, 39 out of 39 Brechin species; Figure S1) while still retaining the ecological information necessary to identify crinoid niche occupation. Further, while the Bromide and Brechin both constitute unusually well-preserved crinoid faunas compared to most, use of this preservation threshold in future studies should maximize the number of faunas to which these methods can be confidently applied.

3.2 Analyses

Analyses were conducted in R version 4.1.0 (R Core Team, 2021). R packages used for analyses were cluster (Maechler, 2019), vegan (Oksanen et al., 2020), paleotree (Bapst, 2012), phytools (Revell, 2012), phangorn (Schliep et al., 2021), geiger (Harmon et al., 2008), and ape (Paradis et al., 2004). All R scripts and data needed to reproduce analyses are provided in the online supplemental materials.

3.2.1 Ecomorphospace Occupation

The vetted datasets of 10 measured characters, which included all taxa with at least partial arms preserved, were combined for the Bromide and Brechin faunas, and a dissimilarity matrix for the dataset was calculated using Gower's coefficient. A principal coordinates analysis (PCO) was then conducted for the resulting dissimilarity matrix, and the major axes were plotted to visualize ecomorphospace occupation of the two faunas. To interpret major sources of variation from the PCO, Spearman's rank correlation tests were used to evaluate dominant associations between PCO scores and ecomorphologic traits, including both measured and calculated traits. To visualize shifts in ecomorphospace occupation between faunas, we used the PCO scores to calculate centroids and visualize their positions on ecomorphospace plots. Centroids were calculated for each fauna as a whole as well as for subclasses Camerata and Pentacrinoidea.

3.2.2 Disparity

Disparity, which captures the diversity of morphological forms, is a valuable tool for investigating evolutionary dynamics that has been widely applied to the crinoid fossil record (Deline, 2021). Although disparity is most commonly calculated for whole organisms to characterize morphological variation across the entire body plan, it can also be measured for subsets of traits in order to test hypotheses concerning different body regions or different types of traits (Ciampaglio, 2002; Deline & Ausich, 2017). Suites of ecomorphological traits are often used to evaluate the diversity of ecological or functional forms, either in isolation or with the goal of explicitly comparing and contrasting functional disparity with total disparity (Anderson, 2009; Mitchell & Mackovicky, 2014; Grossnickle & Newham, 2016; Benevento et al., 2019; Cole & Hopkins, 2021). Here, the ecomorphological traits collected for the Bromide and Brechin crinoid faunas were used to quantify ecological variability within both assemblages. We conducted a series of disparity analyses to further evaluate (1) ecomorphological disparity of crinoids from the Bromide and (2) changes in disparity between the Bromide and Brechin faunas. Dissimilarity matrices and PCOs were calculated separately for each fauna and used to calculate three common disparity indices that capture different facets of morphological disparity: (1) sum of ranges (SOR), which reflects the total amount of morphospace occupied; (2) sum of variances (SOV), which provides a measure of dispersion of taxa around the centroid of the group; and (3) mean pairwise dissimilarity, which summarizes the average distance between all possible taxon pairs and is typically very similar to SOV (Ciampaglio, 2002; Lloyd, 2016; Hopkins & Gerber, 2017). To investigate patterns of disparity at different taxonomic scales, we calculated the three disparity indices for each fauna as a whole and for major groups in each fauna. Groups evaluated were subclass Camerata and its constituent subtaxa (order Diplobathrida, order Monobathrida, and "stem" eucamerates) and subclass Pentacrinoida and its constituent major subtaxa (parvclass Disparida, magnorder Eucladida, suborder Porocrinoidea [porocrinids + hybocrinids], and suborder Flexibilia), based on the revised classification of Wright et al. (2017). Although the genus *Cleiocrinus* has long been classified as a diplobathrid camerate, this affinity has been questioned on the basis of many atypical features, including the absence of interray plates that are considered a synapomorphy of Camerata (Ubaghs, 1978; Cole, 2018). As a result, we included *Cleiocrinus* in measures of total faunal disparity, but excluded it when calculating disparity for diplobathrids. Because disparity indices can only be calculated from samples with two or more taxa, it was not possible to calculate disparity in the Bromide fauna for monobathrids (one species), "stem" eucamerates (one species), or flexibles (no species present).

To further evaluate changes in disparity between the Bromide and the Brechin faunas, we calculated relative disparity for all major groups by dividing the disparity of the group of interest within a fauna by total disparity of the fauna. We also calculated change in relative disparity for all groups with at least two taxa per fauna by subtracting the relative disparity of a group in the Brechin from the relative disparity of the same group in the Bromide. Statistical significance for (1) change in disparity between the Bromide and Brechin faunas and (2) change in relative disparity between groups was calculated for 1,000 bootstrap replications, where taxa in the group of interest were resampled with replacement.

3.2.3 Ecological Clustering and Tree-Based Analyses

Multivariate cluster and phylogeny-based analyses were conducted for the Bromide fauna using the same methods previously applied to the Brechin fauna (Cole et al., 2019). Recent work has resulted in relatively well-resolved phylogenies of Ordovician crinoids at the genus level (Ausich et al., 2015; Cole, 2017b, 2018; Wright, 2017a, 2017b; Wright et al., 2017; Ausich, 2018), and we used these existing phylogenetic hypotheses as a framework to construct an informal tree topology for crinoid genera in the Bromide fauna (Figure 2). Generic relationships that were ambiguous based on previous analyses were left as polytomies at the level of the least inclusive clade. Because species-level phylogenetic hypotheses do not exist for the taxa considered, species were appended onto the genus-level tree assuming monophyly of genera, with species collapsed into polytomies in instances where three or more species were present within a genus. To avoid conditioning results on a single tree topology and set of branch lengths (Soul and Wright, 2021), we used the *cal3* method in the R package paleotree to randomly resolve polytomies from the informal tree topology and produce a set of fully resolved, time-scaled trees (Bapst, 2012, 2013). This procedure uses an a posteriori probabilistic time-scaling approach that draws node ages from a probability distribution based on diversification and sampling rate estimates (Foote, 1997; sampling rate = 0.05, extinction rate = 1.3, origination rate = 1.3; see Cole et al., 2019 for additional details and R code). The procedure was repeated 500 times to produce a set of time-scaled trees that reflect uncertainty in both tree topologies and branch lengths that were used in subsequent tree-based analyses.

To evaluate ecological similarity among taxa, the vetted ecomorphological dataset that included all taxa with at least partial arms was subsetted to include

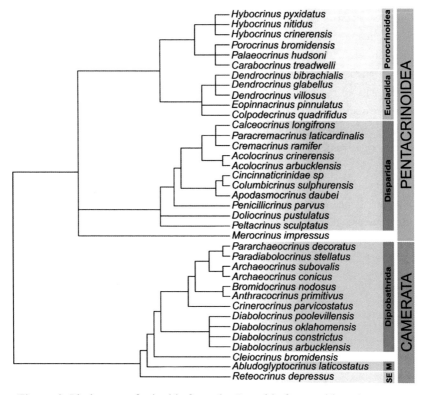

Figure 2 Phylogeny of crinoids from the Bromide fauna with major groups identified. The informal species-level tree topology was constructed using a framework of existing genus-level phylogenies for fossil crinoids (Ausich et al., 2015; Cole, 2017b, 2018; Wright, 2017a, 2017b; Wright et al., 2017; Ausich, 2018). SE = "stem eucamerates," M = Monobathrida.

only Bromide taxa and normalized by making the margin sum of squares equal to one (Oksanen et al., 2020). A dissimilarity matrix was calculated from the normalized trait data using Gower's coefficient, and a cluster analysis was performed using the Ward method to produce a dendrogram that represents ecological similarity among Bromide crinoids. A co-phylogenetic plot, also known as a tanglegram, was then used to visualize the similarities between ecological clustering and the phylogeny of Bromide fauna crinoids. We employed a Monte Carlo procedure to evaluate whether mismatches between ecological clusters and the phylogeny were statistically different from random. The Robinson–Foulds (RF) distance (Robinson & Foulds, 1981), a measure of similarity between tree topologies, was calculated for empirical data from the Bromide fauna and compared with a null distribution of RF distances calculated from 10,000 simulated tree topologies (Cole et al., 2019).

Because only tree topology is taken into account when calculating RF distances, only the unscaled tree topology (i.e., a cladogram) was used for calculating the observed RF value between ecological clusters and the phylogeny.

To evaluate the phylogenetic structure of ecological similarity, we calculated the phylogenetic signal of major ecomorphological characters. Ecomorphological characters considered were filtration fan density (Ω/cm^2), filtration fan area (in cm^2), and body size (calyx volume in cm^3). Both Pagel's Lambda (λ; Pagel, 1999) and Blomberg's K (Blomberg et al., 2003) were calculated for the three ecomorphological characters over the set of 500 time-scaled phylogenies.

4 Results

4.1 Species Richness and Trait Distributions within Clades

There are several notable differences between the Bromide and Brechin assemblages relating to overall faunal composition and species richness of major taxonomic groups (Figure 3). First, flexibles are absent from the Bromide fauna but are represented by three species in the Brechin. In fact, the *Cupulocrinus*-Flexibilia lineage is by far the most numerically abundant group within the Brechin fauna due to the large number of *Cupulocrinus humilis* specimens (Brett & Taylor, 1999; Wright et al., 2019; Cole et al., 2020). Diplobathrids and disparids are the most species-rich groups in the Bromide formation with 12 and 11 species, respectively, but the richness of both groups decreases by about half in the Brechin fauna (Figure 3). By contrast, monobathrid camerates are represented by only a single nominal species in the Bromide but increase to seven species in the Brechin. For stem eucamerates, eucladids, and porocrinoids, species richness is similar, or in some cases identical, between faunas (Figure 3).

Boxplots summarizing variation in filtration fan area, filtration fan density, and body size for clades within each fauna further highlight some substantial differences between faunas (Figure 3). Across all three of these measures in the Bromide fauna, diplobathrids consistently have the highest median values as well as the greatest range of variation. By contrast in the Brechin fauna, both monobathrids and flexibles surpass diplobathrids in terms of median fan area, and many other groups also show notable increases in fan area. Although diplobathrids retain the highest median fan density and body size, both these measures expand dramatically in monobathrids and result in a range that exceeds that of diplobathrids (Figure 3).

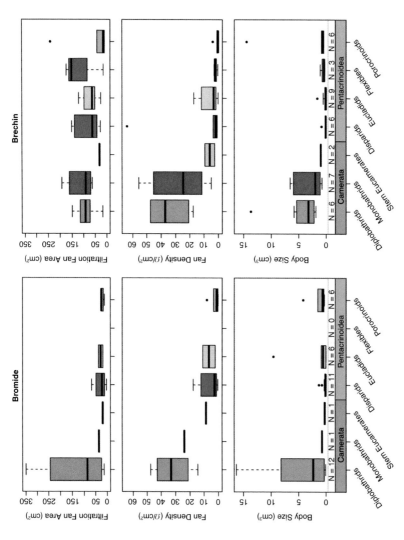

Figure 3 Boxplots comparing fan area, fan density, and body size for the Bromide fauna (left panels) and the Brechin fauna (right panels). Note that flexible crinoids are absent from the Bromide fauna. An outlier for Bromide diplobathrid body size is not shown for plotting purposes (outlier body size = 27.57 cm³). Known species diversity (N) of each group is given at the bottom of the panels.

4.2 Ecomorphospace Occupation

Full results of correlations between traits and the first three PCOs are given in the supplemental materials (Figures S2–S4). The first three PCO axes account for 36.36%, 17.28%, and 13.62% of variation in the dataset respectively, encompassing 67.26% of variation in total. Interpretations of PCO axes based on Spearman's rank correlations with traits are broadly comparable to those made of the Brechin fauna (Cole et al., 2019). The first PCO axis is significantly correlated with all but one trait (brachial width), suggesting PCO 1 strongly reflects aspects of both filtration fan density and size. The second PCO axis correlates almost exclusively with traits related to calyx and fan size, such as arm length, calyx volume, and fan area. The third PCO axis is significantly correlated only with traits tied to feeding ecology, including the number of arm openings, arm branching, and traits tied to brachial and pinnule size. Notably, it is not significantly correlated with filtration fan density or total number of feeding appendages, which suggests PCO 3 reflects components of feeding ecology other than fan density, such as food size selectivity.

Taxa from the Bromide fauna fall into two distinct regions of ecomorphospace that are strongly divided along the first PCO axis and correspond to subclasses Camerata and Pentacrinoidea (Figure 4A). The only exception to this pattern is *Reteocrinus*, a member of a morphologically atypical camerate lineage, which plots within the pentacrinoid region of ecomorphospace. Within the regions occupied by subclasses, there is extensive overlap between subclades, especially for the pentacrinoids. The overall region of ecomorphospace occupation is also larger for pentacrinoids than for camerates.

Ecomorphospace occupation of the Bromide fauna is very similar to that of the Brechin fauna, in that camerates and pentacrinoids from the Brechin are divided into almost nonoverlapping regions of ecomorphospace along the first PCO axis (Figure 4). Again, the only exceptions to this pattern are the stem eucamerate species belonging to the genus *Reteocrinus*. Aside from the stem eucamerates, the separation between the camerate and pentacrinoid regions of ecomorphospace is much more pronounced in the Brechin fauna than in the Bromide, particularly along the first PCO axis (Figure 4). Further, both camerates and pentacrinoids from the Bromide occupy a large range of variation along the second PCO axis, whereas in the Brechin, camerates are restricted to a relatively narrow range along PCO 2 and pentacrinoids maintain a broad distribution along PCO 2.

Centroids for the Bromide at the scale of the whole fauna as well as for subclasses differ only marginally from those for the Brechin fauna (Figure 4). Between the Bromide and Brechin faunas, centroids for the faunas as a whole and for camerate and pentacrinoid subclasses shift slightly toward more negative values

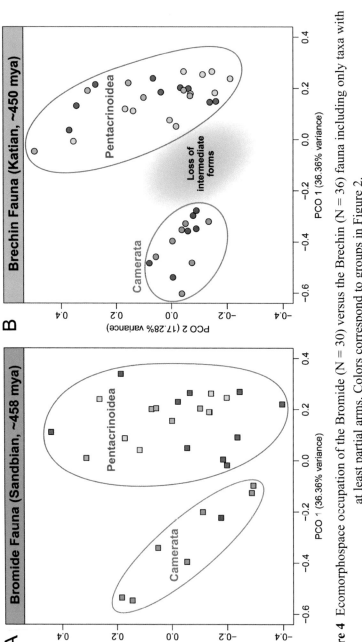

Figure 4 Ecomorphospace occupation of the Bromide (N = 30) versus the Brechin (N = 36) fauna including only taxa with at least partial arms. Colors correspond to groups in Figure 2.

along PCO1 and shift toward more positive values along PCO2 (Figure 5A). Along PCO3, values increase very slightly for camerates, decrease slightly for pentacrinoids, but remain nearly identical between faunas as a whole (Figure 5).

4.3 Disparity

Generally, disparity is greater among clades in the Bromide fauna than in the Brechin (Table 1). Porocrinoids are the only group that consistently goes against this trend, with all three disparity indices increasing from the Bromide to the Brechin. Disparity for all other subclades is consistently lower in the Brechin than the Bromide, regardless of the disparity index considered. For the two faunas as a whole, MPD increases slightly in the Brechin, presumably as a result of the major increase in porocrinoid disparity (Table 1). However, neither the increase in MPD between faunas nor the decreases in SOV or SOR are statistically significant ($p = 0.54$, 0.48, and 0.2, respectively; Figure S5).

Disparity patterns of major crinoid groups are further reinforced by evaluation of relative disparity patterns among subclades but also reveal additional dynamics that are masked at higher taxonomic levels (Figures 6–7). As with raw disparity measures, relative disparity decreases across all groups except for porocrinoids. Within the camerate subclass, the decrease is not significant for camerates as a whole but is statistically significant for diplobathrids across all three disparity indices (Table 2). Likewise, disparity decreases in the pentacrinoid subclass are not statistically significant for pentacrinoids as a whole or for eucladids. In disparids, the decrease in the SOR disparity index is statistically significant, but changes in the other two indices are not. Finally, the disparity increase recovered for porocrinoids is statistically significant across all three indices (Figures 6–7, Table 2).

4.4 Ecological Clustering and Phylogenetic Structure of the Bromide Fauna

Comparison of the phylogeny of the Bromide fauna (Figure 2) with the dendrogram resulting from the cluster analysis reveals many similarities between the two when visualized as a tanglegram (Figure 8). The Robinson–Foulds distance between the cluster analysis and the phylogeny was significantly shorter ($p = 0.043$) than the distances calculated between the cluster analysis and a distribution of 10,000 random trees (Figure S6), indicating that the ecological structure of the Bromide fauna is more similar to the underlying phylogeny than would be expected by chance. A similar pattern was previously recovered in the Brechin fauna (Cole et al., 2019)

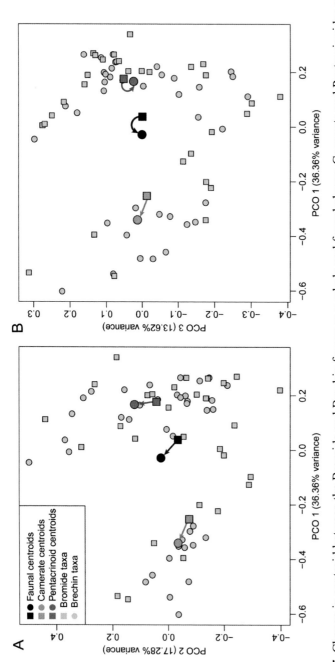

Figure 5 Change in centroid between the Bromide and Brechin faunas as a whole and for subclasses Camerata and Pentacrinoidea across (A) PCO1 and PCO2, and (B) PCO1 and PCO3. Arrows show direction of centroid shifts from the Bromide (large squares) to the Brechin (large circles), and gray points give position of species from the Bromide fauna (squares) and Brechin fauna (circles).

Table 1 Summary of disparity in the Bromide and Brechin faunas across three different disparity indices. Note that monobathrids and stem eucamerates are represented by a single taxon each in the Bromide fauna, and thus disparity indices cannot be calculated for these groups; flexibles are entirely absent from the Bromide fauna. Abbreviations: Subcl. = Subclass, O. = Order, Gr. = Grade, Parv. = Parvclass, Mag. = Magnorder, S.o. = Superorder.

	SOV	SOR	MPD
Bromide (whole fauna)	0.2091	4.6183	0.2263
Subcl. Camerata	0.1787	3.2023	0.1947
O. Diplobathrida	0.1768	2.8603	0.1881
O. Monobathrida	NA	NA	NA
Gr. Stem eucamerates	NA	NA	NA
Subcl. Pentacrinoidea	0.1690	3.9878	0.1902
Parv. Disparida	0.2057	3.8593	0.2129
Mag. Eucladida	0.1503	2.4120	0.1819
S.o. Porocrinoidea	0.0885	1.8334	0.1360
S.o. Flexibilia	NA	NA	NA
Brechin (whole fauna)	0.1818	4.2056	0.2323
Subcl. Camerata	0.0964	2.6141	0.1657
O. Diplobathrida	0.0908	2.0350	0.1499
O. Monobathrida	0.0436	1.3432	0.1306
Gr. Stem eucamerates	0.0074	0.2886	0.0296
Subcl. Pentacrinoidea	0.1299	3.4897	0.1772
Parv. Disparida	0.1140	2.2266	0.1708
Mag. Eucladida	0.0926	2.1379	0.1465
S.o. Porocrinoidea	0.1264	2.4521	0.1679
S.o. Flexibilia	0.0670	1.1796	0.1222

The two phylogenetic signal measures, Pagel's λ and Blomberg's K, both produced similar results when calculated over a distribution of 500 time-scaled trees (Table 3, Figure S7). Significant phylogenetic signal was not recovered for body size or fan area using either of the phylogenetic signal measures, with distributions centered well below 1 in all cases. By contrast, fan density had significant phylogenetic signal for both Pagel's λ and Blomberg's K, with significant p-values recovered for 100 percent of the trees (Table 3). These results differ somewhat from those previously recovered for the Brechin fauna, where both fan density and body size were found to express significant phylogenetic signal, but fan area did not (Cole et al., 2019). As a result, the main difference in phylogenetic structuring of these traits between faunas relates to body size, which occurs in the Brechin but not the Bromide.

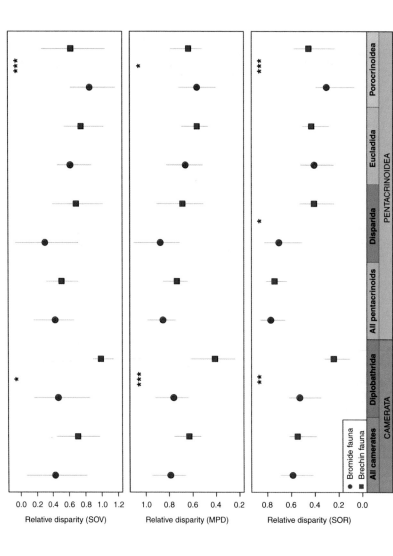

Figure 6 Relative disparity in the Bromide versus Brechin faunas. Relative disparity is calculated by dividing disparity of subgroups in each fauna by the total disparity of the fauna. Plotted points are means from 1,000 bootstrap replications, and error bars reflect the 95 percent confidence intervals generated from bootstrap results. Disparity indices calculated are sum of variances (SOV), mean pairwise dissimilarity (MPD), and sum of ranges (SOR). Asterisks indicate groups for which changes in disparity between the Bromide and Brechin faunas are statistically significant (*$p < 0.05$, **$p < 0.01$, ***$p < 0.001$).

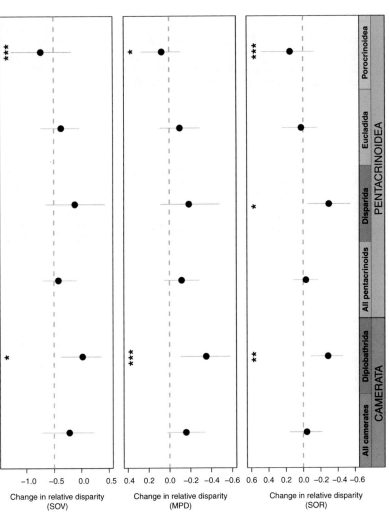

Figure 7 Change in relative disparity between the Bromide and Brechin faunas. Change in relative disparity is calculated by subtracting relative Bromide disparity from relative Brechin disparity (see Figure 6 for relative disparity of each fauna). Values falling above zero (horizontal line) indicate increasing relative disparity through time, whereas those falling below zero indicate decreasing relative disparity. Asterisks indicate groups for which changes in disparity are statistically significant (*$p < 0.05$, ** $p < 0.01$, *** $p < 0.001$).

Table 2 Summary *p*-values for change in relative disparity between the Bromide and Brechin faunas. Statistically significant changes ($p < 0.05$) are denoted by asterisks. Clade abbreviations are the same as for Table 1.

	SOV	SOR	MPD
Subcl. Camerata	0.131	0.245	0.178
O. Diplobathrida	*0.005	*0.001	*0.000
Subcl. Pentacrinoidea	0.350	0.251	0.068
Parv. Disparida	0.089	*0.003	0.051
Mag. Eucladida	0.206	0.654	0.383
S.o. Porocrinoidea	*< 0.000	*< 0.000	*0.014

Table 3 Phylogenetic signal summary statistics for the Bromide fauna calculated over a distribution of trees.

	Fan density	Fan area	Body size
Pagel's λ			
Mean λ	0.978	0.002	0.449
Mean *p*-value	**2.4×10^{-3}**	0.991	0.089
% *p*-value < 0.05	100%	0%	23%
Blomberg's K			
Mean K	1.259	0.442	0.591
Mean *p*-value	**1.8×10^{-3}**	0.717	0.106
% p-value < 0.05	100%	0%	40%

5 Discussion

5.1 Niche Occupation in Upper Ordovician Crinoid Faunas

Overall, crinoid niche occupation is very similar between the Bromide and Brechin faunas. Although the present Element combines the two assemblages for multivariate analyses, patterns of niche occupation recovered for the Brechin fauna are consistent with those from a previous investigation that considered the Brechin in isolation (Cole et al., 2019: Figure 4), indicating that the same major axes of niche differentiation are recovered when the Bromide and Brechin faunas are combined. These axes predominantly correspond to traits that are tied to many aspects of food particle capture like filtration fan density and food size selectivity (Ausich, 1980; Kitazawa et al., 2007) as

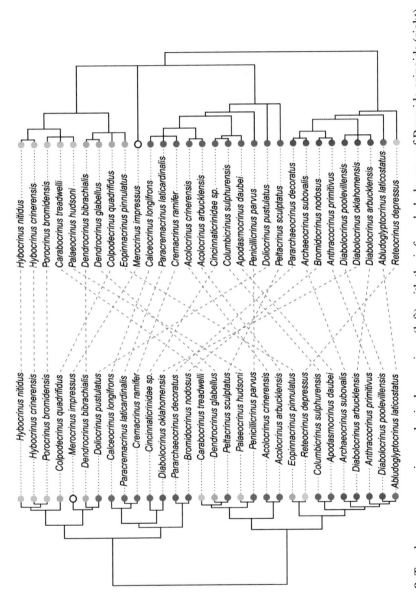

Figure 8 Tanglegram comparing ecological groupings (left) with the inferred phylogeny of Bromide crinoids (right).

well as body size. Within the Bromide fauna, the subclasses Pentacrinoidea and Camerata are clearly divided into two regions of ecomorphospace along the first PCO axis (Figure 4A); this division of ecomorphospace is also observed for the Brechin fauna (Figure 4B). The one exception to this division between camerates and pentacrinoids is *Reteocrinus*, which plots within the pentacrinoid region of ecomorphospace for both faunas. *Reteocrinus* is a morphologically divergent camerate that belongs to the "stem eucamerate" group (sensu Cole, 2017b) that is phylogenetically basal to orders Monobathrid and Diplobathrid. From an ecomorphological perspective, other camerates are united by the presence of pinnulate arms that results in high filtration fan density. By contrast, *Reteocrinus* has apinnulate arms, which is atypical for camerate crinoids and makes the ecomorphology of this genus more similar to that of certain pentacrinoid taxa (i.e., lower filtration fan density). Thus, its affinity within the pentacrinoid region of niche space is unique among camerate crinoids but predictable given its filtration fan morphology.

The strong division of ecomorphospace occupation at the subclass level indicates clade membership plays an important role in niche differentiation. Further, tree-based analyses of Bromide crinoids reveal that ecological clusters are significantly correlated with phylogeny ($p = 0.04$, Figures 8, S6). A similar result was previously recovered for Brechin crinoids (Cole et al., 2019), which indicates that phylogenetic control on niche occupation is a recurring pattern among Upper Ordovician crinoid communities. Significant phylogenetic signal in terms of both Pagel's λ and Blomberg's K is recovered for filtration fan density of Bromide crinoids, but not for fan area or body size (Table 3, Figure S7). Additionally, the mean Blomberg's K value for fan density is greater than 1, indicating that fan density exhibits niche retention in addition to phylogenetic signal. Niche retention is a type of phylogenetic niche conservatism where traits of closely related species are more similar than would be expected given evolutionary models of diffusion through morphospace, which can suggest that the trait(s) in question are subject to constraints or stabilizing selection (Blomberg et al., 2003; Cooper et al., 2010). By comparison, in the Brechin fauna evidence for niche retention was recovered for both filtration fan density and body size, but fan area did not exhibit phylogenetic signal. Combined, these results indicate that among Upper Ordovician crinoid communities, (1) filtration fan density consistently exhibits niche retention, (2) phylogenetic structuring of body size is variable, and (3) fan area is not controlled by phylogeny.

5.2 Crinoid Niche Evolution during the Upper Ordovician

Analyses characterizing patterns of niche occupation and phylogenetic structure reveal many similarities between the Bromide and Brechin faunas. However, further investigations of ecomorphospace occupation and ecological disparity at different taxonomic scales provide deeper insight into patterns of crinoid niche evolution during the Upper Ordovician. Although ecomorphospace occupation is broadly similar between the two faunas, separation between the pentacrinoid and camerate regions of morphospace increased in the Brechin paleocommunity, especially along the first PCO axis, due to an apparent loss of intermediate forms (Figure 4B). This left behind a noticeable gap in ecomorphospace and suggests that increasing specialization and niche differentiation occurred within subclasses during this time. Despite the loss of these intermediate forms, shifts in centroid are relatively minor for the communities as a whole and for individual subclasses (Figure 5). In addition, the overall regions of niche space occupied by camerate and pentacrinoid subclasses both appear to shrink through time (Figure 4). This is further reflected by decreases in SOR, which here measures the total amount of trait space occupied over all PCO axes (Table 1). Other indices measuring different facets of ecological disparity (SOV, MPD) also decrease for both whole communities and subclasses, revealing that the dispersion of taxa around the centroid and the proximity of taxa to each other in niche space decrease through time as well, although these decreases are not statistically significant (Table 2, Figures 6–7). Combined, these results establish that ecological stasis is the dominant pattern apparent at high taxonomic scales over the study interval. In other words, the major ecological strategies were broadly conserved along clade membership lines. However, increasing separation of adaptive zones between subclasses (and within-group decreases in ecological disparity) suggest a trend of increasing niche differentiation across most major crinoid groups during the Late Ordovician, potentially driven by competition avoidance.

Although nonstatistically significant decreases in ecological disparity are widespread at high taxonomic levels (e.g., whole communities and subclasses), they mask notable shifts occurring at lower taxonomic levels. In contrast to most groups that undergo only minor shifts in disparity, Porocrinoidea and Diplobathrida stand out as the only groups for which statistically significant changes in disparity occur through time across all disparity indices (Figures 6–7, Table 2). Porocrinoids are the only group for which a statistically significant *increase* in disparity through time is consistently recovered (Figures 6–7). This increase in porocrinoid disparity cannot be due to sample size alone, because equal numbers of porocrinoid taxa are sampled for both the Bromide and Brechin paleocommunities. Instead, the adaptive zone of porocrinoids appears to have expanded during this time, resulting in both a greater amount of occupied niche space and an increased ecological distance between individual species. The most notable outlier responsible for the expansion of porocrinoid ecomorphospace is *Carabocrinus vancourtlandti*, which is particularly notable for its large body size. Diplobathrids are the only group for which a significant *decrease* in disparity through time is consistently recovered (Figures 6–7). Although diplobathrid richness decreases from twelve to six species in the communities compared, only seven of the Bromide species are included in disparity calculations due to preservational vetting, so richness/sample size alone is not sufficient to account for this significant drop in disparity. Additionally, the disparity of Brechin camerates as a whole (monobathrids, diplobathrids, and stem eucamerates combined) is lower than that of Bromide diplobathrids, despite the fact that camerate species richness is far greater in the Brechin paleocommunity from the addition of many new monobathrid species. This suggests that camerate niche occupation became increasingly constrained during the Upper Ordovician, with the ecology of newly evolved species deviating only minimally from that of ancestral forms. Further, it suggests diplobathrids were subjected to increasing ecological competition during the Upper Ordovician as monobathrids diversified within overlapping areas of niche space.

5.3 Transition between the Early and Middle Crinoid Evolutionary Faunas

The evolutionary history of Paleozoic crinoids has been divided into the early, middle, and late Paleozoic Crinoid Evolutionary Faunas (CEFs), each of which were dominated by different groups of crinoids (Baumiller, 1994; Ausich et al., 1994). The transition between the early and middle Paleozoic CEFs occurred around the close of the Ordovician and resulted in a shift from crinoid communities dominated by disparids, diplobathrid camerates, and hybocrinids to one characterized by monobathrid camerates, flexibles, and "primitive" cladids (Ausich & Deline, 2012). Traditionally, this major faunal transition is thought to be concomitant with the Late Ordovician mass extinction, an event that resulted in significant loss of crinoid genera at the end of the Katian stage due to glacially induced, eustatic sea level fall (Peters & Ausich, 2008). As a result, the Late Ordovician mass extinction has been considered the trigger for this shift between evolutionary faunas, with heterogeneity in clades' extinction severity and postextinction recovery leading to changes in dominance. However, there is also some evidence that faunal composition had begun to shift during late Sandbian–early Katian, several million years before the end of the Katian (Ausich & Deline, 2012). Evaluation of trends in both richness and ecological disparity of Bromide and Brechin crinoid faunas provides further insight into ecological drivers of this transition during its early stages.

The taxonomic composition of the Bromide and Brechin faunas is broadly consistent with the expected early CEF makeup of abundant disparids, diploba-thrid camerates, and hybocrinids. However, notable decreases in species rich-ness of both diplobathrids and disparids occur between the two faunas, while both flexible and monobathrid crinoids – groups that define the middle CEF – increase in species richness from the Bromide to Brechin (Figure 3). Similarly, the geologically younger Brechin fauna contains fewer hybocrinid species than the Bromide. Although smaller in magnitude, these patterns broadly parallel Late Ordovician to middle Silurian trends in increasing versus declining species richness that occur, especially within those crinoid groups that define the early and middle CEFs (Ausich & Deline, 2012). In addition, both diplobathrids and disparids experienced statistically significant decreases in ecological disparity through time between the Bromide and Brechin faunas. This suggests that decreases in overall ecological variation occurred within these groups, and niche evolution became increasingly constrained within shrinking adaptive zones. Because ecological variation can serve as a major driver for speciation, it is possible that these decreases in ecological disparity reduced origination propensity within subclades, whereas the evolution and diversification of phylogenetically distant (but ecologically similar) groups may have increased competition. For example, diplobathrids and monobathrids experienced oppos-ite diversification dynamics: diversity and ecological disparity both decreased in diplobathrids but increased in monobathrids. Because of the extensive over-lap between monobathrid and diplobathrid niches, this likely resulted in increased competition pressure on diplobathrids. Overall, these changes in clade richness and ecological disparity between the Bromide and Brechin faunas provide evidence that the transition between CEFs may have begun during the Late Ordovician, well before the mass extinction event. Thus, instead of serving as the trigger of the early to middle CEF transition, the Late Ordovician mass extinction appears to have simply hastened and amplified a faunal transition that was already underway by the Katian (middle Late Ordovician). Large-scale faunal turnover in the absence of global-scale mass extinction is not unprecedented in the geological history of crinoids. Notably, the late Mississippian transition from the middle to the late CEF did not coincide with a mass extinction, but instead was predominantly driven by differences in rates of origination and extinction that were presumably caused by long-term ecological and environmental pressures (Kammer & Ausich, 2006; Sallan et al., 2011; Ausich & Kammer, 2013). Similarly, the Late Ordovician mass extinction may have acted to accelerate the long-term outcome of "background" turnover, at least for crinoids. These results suggest that paleobiologists need not assume that conflicts exist between tiers of ecological and evolutionary processes (Gould, 1985). Instead of investing in false dichotomies, comparisons between patterns at multiple taxonomic, temporal, and spatial scales may be used to determine when and how processes acting at different hierarchical levels may hitchhike, reinforce, or obscure one another (Jablonski 2007). Only then can we build a more synthetic view of the evolution of clades and communities through time.

5.4 Extension of the Niche Differentiation Model to Other Echinoderms

While this Element has focused exclusively on crinoids from the Bromide and Brechin faunas, crinoids would have competed for food resources from a number of other co-occurring filter-feeding organisms, including other echinoderms as well as bryozoans, sponges, and corals. In particular, echinoderm diversity at the class level was especially high during the Ordovician, with at least seventeen classes represented (Sprinkle, 1982a). This class-level diversity is reflected in the broader composition of both the Bromide and Brechin faunas, which contain filter-feeding echinoderms like paracrinoids, rhombiferans, and eocrinoids in addition to crinoids (Brett & Liddel, 1978; Sprinkle, 1982a). These echinoderms would have played significant roles within paleocommunities due to their abundance (either locally or throughout the study sections), and some may have been in direct competition with crinoids for food, given similarities in their feeding apparatus. For example, paracrinoids are found throughout the Bromide Formation and make up over 97 percent of echinoderm fossils recovered from the upper Echinoderm Zone, the overwhelming majority of which belong to *Oklahomacystis* (Parsley, 1982a; Sprinkle, 1982b). The diploporitan *Eumorphocystis multiporata* is also very abundant in the Bromide and is notable in that the construction of its filtration fan is similar to that of crinoids (Parsley, 1982b; Sprinkle, 1982b). Filter-feeding echinoderms other than crinoids are less common in the Brechin but are still represented by a large number of taxa, including edrioblastoids, rhombiferans, and paracrinoids (Brett & Liddel, 1978).

Given that other filter-feeding echinoderms were diverse, abundant, and may have had niches that overlapped with those of crinoids during the Ordovician, it would be ideal to investigate feeding ecology across all these echinoderm groups in order to evaluate niche partitioning and competition at the class level. However, a number of challenges must be surmounted before the approaches to niche differentiation that have been applied to crinoids in this

Element can be generalized to other echinoderms. First, the feeding mode for some echinoderms is not always clear, and thus care must be taken in determining which echinoderms are filter feeders (e.g., Gorzelak & Zamora, 2016). Second, construction of the feeding apparatus varies widely across filter-feeding echinoderms. Many do not have arms or brachioles positioned in circular fans like crinoids, but instead may have them positioned in a single row (e.g., *Amygdalocystis*; Guensburg, 1991), in multiple rows along the theca or other various positions relating to the ambulacra (e.g., rhombiferans; Sumrall & Shumacher, 2002), or lack skeletonized feeding appendages entirely (e.g., edrioblastoids; Sprinkle, 1982c). As a result, concepts like fan density and fan area that are key for crinoid niche characterization and differentiation do not necessarily apply to other echinoderms. A final challenge is a taphonomic one, where the feeding structures of many echinoderms are much more delicate than those of crinoids (Guensburg, 1991; Brett et al., 1997). As a result, these structures are only very rarely preserved, making it much more difficult to adequately sample a representative cross section of taxa from any given fauna. Despite these challenges, it is clear that other filter-feeding echinoderms were significant components of ecological communities, especially during the Ordovician when class-level diversity was very high. Thus, more fully characterizing the niches of all filter-feeding echinoderms and evaluating ecological dynamics between clades remains an exciting area for future study.

6 Conclusions

This Element leverages the extensive amount of ecological data contained within the crinoid fossil record to evaluate patterns of community paleoecology, niche occupation, and niche evolution across the two most diverse and well-studied crinoid assemblages known from the Upper Ordovician: the Bromide fauna from the Sandbian of Oklahoma and the Brechin fauna from the Katian of Ontario. The same major axes of niche differentiation – fan density, food size selectivity, and body size – are recovered in the Bromide fauna as were previously recovered for the Brechin, suggesting these traits consistently delineated crinoid niches during the Upper Ordovician. Tree-based analyses of both the Bromide and Brechin faunas further reveal that niche occupation was heavily influenced by phylogeny throughout the Upper Ordovician, with subclasses Camerata and Pentacrinoidea exhibiting almost nonoverlapping adaptive zones. At a faunal-level scale, niche distributions did not change extensively over the study interval, indicating general ecological stasis over a time period of < 5 million years. At the subclass level, however, crinoid niches became increasingly specialized and differentiated during this time, as revealed by increasing separation between regions of occupied niche space, decreases in total amount of niche space occupied, and increased species packing within occupied regions of ecomorphospace. Relatively minor decreases in ecological disparity also occurred at most higher taxonomic scales, suggesting a general trend of increased niche differentiation over the study interval. However, the patterns observed at higher taxonomic scales mask significant changes in disparity that occurred within porocrinoids, diplobathrids, and disparids, highlighting the importance of conducting these types of investigations at multiple scales in order to better capture dynamics occurring at different hierarchical levels.

Changes in both species richness and ecological disparity of major crinoid groups in the Bromide and Brechin faunas are consistent with the transition between the early and middle Paleozoic Crinoid Evolutionary Faunas. In particular, richness and disparity decreased in groups like diplobathrids and disparids but increased in groups like monobathrids and flexibles. These patterns reveal that the shift between CEFs was underway by at least the Katian, well before the onset of the Late Ordovician mass extinction that has been considered the trigger of the early to middle CEF transition. Instead, these results provide evidence that suggests the early to middle CEF transition initially began as a result of ecological drivers, and the Late Ordovician mass extinction served to intensify and/or speed up the timing of this transition. The role of ecological drivers in the generation and maintenance of macroevolutionary patterns is often obscured in the fossil record due to overprinting by environmental phenomena, such as mass extinction events. This Element highlights the importance of using phylogenetic and other quantitative methods to study ecological phenomena in deep time, including identifying axes of niche differentiation, the control that phylogeny exerts on niche occupation, time frames over which niches evolve versus remaining static, and the role of ecology in major faunal transitions.

6.1 Supporting Materials

Supplemental methods, figures, and data and R scripts needed to reproduce analyses are available at: www.cambridge.org/colewright.

References

Anderson, P. S. (2009). Biomechanics, functional patterns, and disparity in Late Devonian arthrodires. *Paleobiology*, **35**(3), 321–342.

Andrews, P., Lord, J. M., & Evans, E. M. N. (1979). Patterns of ecological diversity in fossil and modern mammalian faunas. *Biological Journal of the Linnean Society*, **11**(2), 177–205.

Antell, G. S., Fenton, I. S., Valdes, P. J., & Saupe, E. E. (2021). Thermal niches of planktonic foraminifera are static throughout glacial–interglacial climate change. *Proceedings of the National Academy of Sciences*, **118**(18), e2017105118.

Armstrong, D. K. (2000). Paleozoic geology of the northern Lake Simcoe area, south-central Ontario. *Ontario Geological Survey, Open File Report*, **6011**, pp. 1–43.

Ausich, W. I. (1980). A model for niche differentiation in Lower Mississippian crinoid communities. *Journal of Paleontology*, **54**(2), 273–288.

Ausich, W. I. (1983). Component concept for the study of the paleocommunities with an example from the Early Carboniferous of Southern Indiana (USA). *Palaeogeography, Palaeoclimatology, Palaeoecology*, **44**(3–4), 251–282.

Ausich, W. I. (2001). Echinoderm taphonomy. In M. Jangoux and J. M. Lawrence, eds., *Echinoderm Studies 6*. A. A. Balkema, Rotterdam, pp. 171–227.

Ausich, W. I. (2016). Fossil species as data: a perspective from echinoderms. In W. D. Allmon and M. M. Yacobucci, eds., *Species and Speciation in the Fossil Record*. University of Chicago Press, Chicago, pp. 301–311.

Ausich, W. I. (2018). Morphological paradox of disparid crinoids (Echinodermata): phylogenetic analysis of a Paleozoic clade. *Swiss Journal of Palaeontology*, **137**(2), 159–176.

Ausich, W. I. (2021). Disarticulation and Preservation of Fossil Echinoderms: Recognition of Ecological-Time Information in the Echinoderm Fossil Record. *Elements of Paleontology*. Cambridge University Press, Cambridge, UK.

Ausich, W. I., & Baumiller, T. K. (1993). Taphonomic method for determining muscular articulations in fossil crinoids. *Palaios*, **8**(5), 477–484.

Ausich, W. I., & Bottjer, D. J. (1982). Tiering in suspension-feeding communities on soft substrata throughout the Phanerozoic. *Science*, **216** (4542), 173–174.

Ausich, W. I., & Deline, B. (2012). Macroevolutionary transition in crinoids following the Late Ordovician extinction event (Ordovician to Early Silurian). *Palaeogeography, Palaeoclimatology, Palaeoecology*, **361–362**, 38–48.

Ausich, W. I., & Kammer, T. W. (2013). Mississippian crinoid biodiversity, biogeography and macroevolution. *Palaeontology*, **56**(4), 727–740.

Ausich, W. I., Kammer, T. W., & Baumiller, T. K. (1994). Demise of the Middle Paleozoic crinoid fauna: a single extinction event or rapid faunal turnover? *Paleobiology*, **20**(3), 345–361.

Ausich, W. I., Kammer, T. W., Rhenberg, E. C., & Wright, D. F. (2015). Early phylogeny of crinoids within the pelmatozoan clade. *Palaeontology*, **58**(6), 937–952.

Ausich, W. I., Wright, D. F., Cole, S. R., & Koniecki, J. M. (2018). Disparid and hybocrinid crinoids (Echinodermata) from the Upper Ordovician (lower Katian) Brechin Lagerstätte of Ontario. *Journal of Paleontology*, **92**(5), 850–871.

Bambach, R. K. (1983). Ecospace utilization and guilds in marine communities through the Phanerozoic. In M. J. S. Tevesz and P. L. McCall, eds., *Biotic Interactions in Recent and Fossil Benthic Communities*. Springer, Boston, pp. 719–746.

Bambach, R. K., Bush, A. M., & Erwin, D. H. (2007). Autecology and the filling of ecospace: key metazoan radiations. *Palaeontology*, **50**(1), 1–22.

Bapst, D. W. (2012). paleotree: an R package for paleontological and phylogenetic analyses of evolution. *Methods in Ecology and Evolution*, **3**(5), 803–807.

Bapst, D. W. (2013). A stochastic rate-calibrated method for time-scaling phylogenies of fossil taxa. *Methods in Ecology and Evolution*, **4**(8), 724–733.

Barr, W. A. (2018). Ecomorphology. In D. A. Croft, D. F. Su, and S. W. Simpson, eds., *Methods in Paleoecology*. Springer, Dordrecht, 339–349.

Baumiller, T. K. (1993). Survivorship analysis of Paleozoic Crinoidea: effect of filter morphology on evolutionary rates. *Paleobiology*, **19**(3), 304–321.

Baumiller, T. K. (1997). Crinoid functional morphology. *Paleontological Society Papers*, **3**, 45–68.

Baumiller, T. K. (2008). Crinoid ecological morphology. *Annual Review of Earth Planetary Sciences*, **36**(1), 221–249.

Baumiller, T. K. (2020). Patterns of dominance and extinction in the record of Paleozoic crinoids. In B. David, A. Guille, J. P. Guille, and M. Roux, eds., *Echinoderms Through Time*. CRC Press, London, pp. 193–198.

Baumiller, T. K., & Ausich, W. I. (1996). Crinoid stalk flexibility: theoretical predictions and fossil stalk postures. *Lethaia*, **29**(1), 47–59.

Baumiller, T. K., & Gahn, F. (2003). Predation on crinoids. In P. H. Kelley, M. Kowalewski, & T. A. Hansen, eds., *Predator-Prey Interactions in the Fossil Record*. Topics in Geobiology, Kluwer Academic/Plenum Publishers, Dordrecht, **20**, 263–278.

Benevento, G.L., Benson, R.B., & Friedman, M. (2019). Patterns of mammalian jaw ecomorphological disparity during the Mesozoic/Cenozoic transition. *Proceedings of the Royal Society B*, **286**(1902), 20190347.

Bennington, J. B., & Bambach, R. K. (1996). Statistical testing for paleocommunity recurrence: are similar fossil assemblages ever the same? *Palaeogeography, Palaeoclimatology, Palaeoecology*, **127**(1–4), 107–133.

Blake, D. B., & Koniecki, J. (2019). Two new Paleozoic Asteroidea (Echinodermata) and their taxonomic and evolutionary significance. *Journal of Paleontology*, **93**(1), 105–114.

Blake, D. B., & Koniecki, J. (2020). Taxonomy and functional morphology of the Urasterellidae (Paleozoic Asteroidea, Echinodermata). *Journal of Paleontology*, **94**(6), 1124–1147.

Blomberg, S. P., Garland Jr., T., & Ives, A. R. (2003). Testing for phylogenetic signal in comparative data: behavioral traits are more labile. *Evolution*, **57**(4), 717–745.

Bock, W. J. (1994). Concepts and methods in ecomorphology. *Journal of Biosciences*, **19**(4), 403–413.

Brame, H. M. R., & Stigall, A. L. (2014). Controls on niche stability in geologic time: congruent responses to biotic and abiotic environmental changes among Cincinnatian (Late Ordovician) marine invertebrates. *Paleobiology*, **40**(1), 70–90.

Brett, C. E., & Liddell, W. D. (1978). Preservation and paleoecology of a Middle Ordovician hardground community. *Paleobiology*, **4**(3), 329–348.

Brett, C. E., Moffat, H. A., & Taylor, W. L. (1997). Echinoderm taphonomy, taphofacies, and Lagerstätten. *Paleontological Society Papers*, **3**, 147–190.

Brett, C. E., & Taylor, W. L. (1999). Middle Ordovician of the Lake Simcoe area of Ontario, Canada. In H. Hess, W. I. Ausich, C. E. Brett, and M. H. Simms, eds, *Fossil Crinoids*. Cambridge University Press, Cambridge, UK, pp. 68–74.

Brower, J. C. (2007). The application of filtration theory to food gathering in Ordovician crinoids. *Journal of Paleontology*, **81**(6), 1284–1300.

Brower, J. C. (2013). Paleoecology of echinoderm assemblages from the Upper Ordovician (Katian) Dunleith Formation of Northern Iowa and Southern Minnesota. *Journal of Paleontology*, **87**(1), 16–43.

Bush, A. M., & Bambach, R. K. (2011). Paleoecologic megatrends in marine metazoa. *Annual Review of Earth and Planetary Sciences*, **39**(1), 241–269.

Carlucci, J. R., Westrop, S. R., Brett, C. E., & Burkhalter, R. (2014). Facies architecture and sequence stratigraphy of the Ordovician Bromide Formation (Oklahoma): a new perspective on a mixed carbonate-siliciclastic ramp. *Facies*, **60**(4), 987–1012.

Carrano, M. T. (1997). Morphological indicators of foot posture in mammals: a statistical and biomechanical analysis. *Zoological Journal of the Linnean Society*, **121**(1), 77–104.

Cavender-Bares, J., Kozak, K. H., Fine, P. V., & Kembel, S. W. (2009). The merging of community ecology and phylogenetic biology. *Ecology Letters*, **12**(7), 693–715.

Chang, L.M. & Skipwith, P.L. (2021). Relatedness and the composition of communities over time: evaluating phylogenetic community structure in the late Cenozoic record of bivalves. *Paleobiology*, **47**(2), 301–313.

Ciampaglio, C. N. (2002). Determining the role that ecological and developmental constraints play in controlling disparity: examples from the crinoid and blastozoan fossil record. *Evolution & Development*, **4**(3), 170–188.

Cole, S. R. (2017a). Phylogeny, Diversification, and Extinction Selectivity in Camerate Crinoids. The Ohio State University, doctoral dissertation.

Cole, S. R. (2017b). Phylogeny and morphologic evolution of the Ordovician Camerata (Class Crinoidea, Phylum Echinodermata). *Journal of Paleontology*, **91**(4), 815–828.

Cole, S. R. (2018). Phylogeny and evolutionary history of diplobathrid crinoids (Echinodermata). *Palaeontology*, **62**(3), 357–373.

Cole, S. R. (2019). Hierarchical controls on extinction selectivity across the diplobathrid crinoid phylogeny. *Paleobiology*, **47**(2), 251–270.

Cole, S. R., Ausich, W. I., Colmenar, J., & Zamora, S. (2017). Filling the Gondwanan gap: paleobiogeographic implications of new crinoids from the Castillejo and Fombuena formations (Middle and Upper Ordovician, Iberian Chains, Spain). *Journal of Paleontology*, **91**(4), 715–734.

Cole, S. R., Ausich, W. I., Wright, D. F., & Koniecki, J. M. (2018). An echinoderm Lagerstätte from the Upper Ordovician (Katian), Ontario: taxonomic re-evaluation and description of new dicyclic camerate crinoids. *Journal of Paleontology*, **92**(3), 488–505.

Cole, S. R., & Hopkins, M. J. (2021). Selectivity and the effect of mass extinctions on disparity and functional ecology. *Science Advances*, **7**(19), eabf4072.

Cole, S. R., Wright, D. F., & Ausich, W. I. (2019). Phylogenetic community paleoecology of one of the earliest complex crinoid faunas (Brechin Lagerstätte, Ordovician). *Palaeogeography, Palaeoclimatology, Palaeoecology*, **521**, 82–98.

Cole, S. R., Wright, D. F., Ausich, W. I., & Koniecki, J. M. (2020). Paleocommunity composition, relative abundance, and new camerate crinoids from the Brechin Lagerstätte (Upper Ordovician). *Journal of Paleontology*, **94**(6), 1103–1123.

Cooper, N., Jetz, W., & Freckleton, R. P. (2010). Phylogenetic comparative approaches for studying niche conservatism. *Journal of Evolutionary Biology*, **23**(12), 2529–2539.

Darroch, S. A., Laflamme, M., & Wagner, P. J. (2018). High ecological complexity in benthic Ediacaran communities. *Nature Ecology & Evolution*, **2**(10), 1541–1547.

Deline, B. (2021). Echinoderm Morphological Disparity: Methods, Patterns, and Possibilities. *Elements of Paleontology*. Cambridge University Press, Cambridge, UK.

Deline, B., & Ausich, W. I. (2011). Testing the plateau: a reexamination of disparity and morphologic constraints in early Paleozoic crinoids. *Paleobiology*, **37**(2), 214–236.

Deline, B., Greenwood, J. M., Clark, J. W. et al. (2018). Evolution of metazoan morphological disparity. *Proceedings of the National Academy of Sciences*, **115**(38), E8909–E8918.

Deline, B., & Thomka, J. R. (2017). The role of preservation on the quantification of morphology and patterns of disparity within Paleozoic echinoderms. *Journal of Paleontology*, **91**(4), 618–632.

Deline, B., Thompson, J. R., Smith, N. S. et al. (2020). Evolution and development at the origin of a phylum. *Current Biology*, **30**(9), 1672–1679.

Dineen, A. A., Fraiser, M. L., & Sheehan, P. M. (2014). Quantifying functional diversity in pre- and post-extinction paleocommunities: a test of ecological restructuring after the end-Permian mass extinction. *Earth-Science Reviews*, **136**, 339–349.

Donovan, S. K. (1991). The taphonomy of echinoderms: calcareous multi-element skeletons in the marine environment. In S. K. Donovan, ed., *The Processes of Fossilization*. Belhaven Press, London, pp. 241–269.

Erwin, D. H. (2008). Macroevolution of ecosystem engineering, niche construction and diversity. *Trends in Ecology & Evolution*, **23**(6), 304–310.

Evans, A. R., & Pineda-Munoz, S. (2018). Inferring mammal dietary ecology from dental morphology. In D. A. Croft, D. F. Su, and S. W. Simpson, eds., *Methods in Paleoecology*. Springer, New York, 37–51.

Feng, Z., Wang, J., Rößler, R., Ślipiński, A., & Labandeira, C. (2017). Late Permian wood-borings reveal an intricate network of ecological relationships. *Nature Communications*, **8**(1), 556.

Fischer, V., Benson, R.B., Zverkov, N.G. et al. (2017). Plasticity and convergence in the evolution of short-necked plesiosaurs. *Current Biology*, **27**(11), 1667–1676.

Foote, M. (1994). Morphological disparity in Ordovician–Devonian crinoids and the early saturation of morphological space. *Paleobiology*, **20**(3), 320–344.

Foote, M. (1997). Estimating taxonomic durations and preservation probability. *Paleobiology*, **23**(3), 278–300.

Foote, M. (1999). Morphological diversity in the evolutionary radiation of Paleozoic and post-Paleozoic crinoids. *Paleobiology*, **25**(S2), 1–115.

Fountain-Jones, N.M., Baker, S.C., & Jordan, G.J. (2014). Moving beyond the guild concept: developing a practical functional trait framework for terrestrial beetles. *Ecological Entomology*, **40**(1), 1–13.

Fraser, D., Gorelick, R., & Rybczynski, N. (2015). Macroevolution & climate change influence phylogenetic community assembly of North American hoofed mammals. *Biological Journal of the Linnean Society*, **114**(3), 485–494.

Fraser, D., & Lyons, S. K. (2017). Biotic interchange has structured Western Hemisphere mammal communities. *Global Ecology and Biogeography*, **26** (12), 1408–1422.

Fraser, D., & Lyons, S. K. (2020). Mammal community structure through the Paleocene-Eocene thermal maximum. *The American Naturalist*, **196**(3), 271–290.

Gibson, B. M., Furbish, D. J., Rahman, I. A. et al. (2021). Ancient life and moving fluids. *Biological Reviews*, **96**(1), 129–152.

Goldman, D., Sadler, P. M., Leslie, S. A. et al. (2020). The Ordovician Period. In F. M. Gradstein, J. M. Ogg, M. D. Schmitz, G. M. Ogg, eds., *Geological Time Scale 2020*. Elsevier, Amsterdam, vol. 2, pp. 631–694.

Gorzelak, P. & Zamora, S. (2016). Understanding form and function of the stem in early flattened echinoderms (pleurocystitids) using a microstructural approach. *PeerJ*, **4**, e1820. doi: https://doi.org/10.7717/peerj.1820

Gould, S. J. (1985). The paradox of the first tier: an agenda for paleobiology. *Paleobiology*, **11**(1), 2–12.

Grossnickle, D.M. & Newham, E. (2016). Therian mammals experience an ecomorphological radiation during the Late Cretaceous and selective extinction at the K–Pg boundary. *Proceedings of the Royal Society B*, **283**(1832), 20160256.

Guensburg, T. E. (1991). The stem and holdfast of *Amygdalocystites florealis* Billings, 1854 (Paracrinoidea): lifestyle implications. *Journal of Paleontology*, **65**(4), 693–695.

Guensburg, T. E., & Sprinkle, J. (2003). The oldest known crinoids (Early Ordovician, Utah) and a new crinoid plate homology system. *Bulletins of American Paleontology*, **364**, 1–43.

Hadly, E. A., Spaeth, P. A. & Li, C. (2009). Niche conservatism above the species level. *Proceedings of the National Academy of Sciences*, **106** (S2), 19707–19714.

Harmon, L. J., Weir, J. T., Brock, C. D., Glor, R. E., & Challenger, W. (2008). GEIGER: investigating evolutionary radiations. *Bioinformatics*, **24**(1), 129–131.

Holland, S. M., & Zaffos, A. (2011). Niche conservatism along an onshore-offshore gradient. *Paleobiology*, **37**(2), 270–286.

Hopkins, M. J., & Gerber, S. (2017). Morphological disparity. In L. N. de la Rosa and G. Müller, eds., *Evolutionary Developmental Biology*. Springer International Publishing, New York, pp. 1–12.

Hutchinson, G. E. (1978). *An Introduction to Population Biology*. Yale University Press, New Haven and London.

Jablonski, D. (2007). Scale and hierarchy in macroevolution. *Palaeontology*, **50** (1), 87–109.

Kammer, T. W. (1985). Aerosol filtration theory applied to Mississippian deltaic crinoids. *Journal of Paleontology*, **59**(3), 551–560.

Kammer, T. W., & Ausich, W. I. (2006). The "Age of Crinoids": A Mississippian biodiversity spike coincident with widespread carbonate ramps. *Palaios*, **21**(3), 238–248.

Kelley, P., Kowalewski, M., & Hansen, T. A. (Eds.). (2003). *Predator-Prey Interactions in the Fossil Record*, Topics in Geobiology **20**, Kluwer Academic/Plenum Publishers, New York.

Kidwell, S. M., & Behrensmeyer, A. K. (Eds). (1993). *Taphonomic Approaches to Time Resolution in the Fossil Assemblages*, Short Courses in Paleontology, **6**, Paleontological Society.

Kitazawa, K., Oji, T., & Sunamura, M. (2007). Food composition of crinoids (Crinoidea: Echinodermata) in relation to stalk length and fan density: their paleoecological implications. *Marine Biology*, **152**(4), 959–968.

Kolata, D. R. (1982). Camerates. In J. Sprinkle, ed., *Echinoderm Faunas from the Bromide Formation (Middle Ordovician) of Oklahoma.* The University of Kansas Paleontological Contributions, Lawrence, **1**, pp. 170–205.

Lamsdell, J.C., Congreve, C.R., Hopkins, M.J., Krug, A.Z., & Patzkowsky, M. E. (2017). Phylogenetic paleoecology: tree-thinking and ecology in deep time. *Trends in Ecology & Evolution*, **32**(6), 452–463.

Liberty, B. A. (1969). Palaeozoic geology of the Lake Simcoe area, Ontario. *Geological Survey of Canada Memoir*, **355**, pp. 1–201.

Lloyd, G. T. (2016). Estimating morphological diversity and tempo with discrete character-taxon matrices: implementation, challenges, progress, and future directions. *Biological Journal of the Linnean Society*, **118**(1), 131–151.

Longman, M. W. (1982). Depositional setting and regional characteristics. In J. Sprinkle, ed., *Echinoderm Faunas from the Bromide Formation (Middle Ordovician) of Oklahoma.* The University of Kansas Paleontological Contributions, Lawrence, **1**, pp. 6–10.

Lyons, S. K., Behrensmeyer, A. K., & Wagner, P. J. (Eds.). (2019). *Foundations of Paleoecology: Classic Papers with Commentaries.* University of Chicago Press, Chicago.

Macurda, D. B., & Meyer, D. L. (1974). Feeding posture of modern stalked crinoids. *Nature*, **247**(5440), 394–396.

Maechler, M., Rousseeuw, P. R., Struyf, A., & Gonzalez, J. (2019). *Finding Groups in Data: Cluster Analysis Extended Rousseeuw et al.* R package version 2.1.2.

Mallon, J. C. (2019). Competition structured a Late Cretaceous megaherbivorous dinosaur assemblage. *Scientific Reports*, **9**(1), 1–18.

Messing, C. G., Hoggett, A. K., Vail, L. L., Rouse, G. W., & Rowe, F. W. E. (2017). 7: Class Crinoidea. In T. O'Hara and M. Byrne, eds., *Australian Echinoderms: Biology, Ecology and Evolution.* Csiro Publishing, Clayton, Australia, pp. 167–225.

Meyer, D. L. (1973). Feeding behavior and ecology of shallow-water unstalked crinoids (Echinodermata) in the Caribbean Sea. *Marine Biology*, **22**(2), 105–129.

Meyer, D. L. (1979). Length and spacing of the tube feet in crinoids (Echinodermata) and their role in suspension-feeding. *Marine Biology*, **51** (4), 361–369.

Meyer, D. L., & Ausich, W. I. (1983). Biotic interactions among recent and among fossil crinoids. In M. J. S. Tevesz & P. L. McCall, eds., *Biotic Interactions in Recent and Fossil Benthic Communities.* Topics in Geobiology, Kluwer Academic/Plenum Publishers, New York, pp. 377–427.

Meyer, D. L., Miller, A. I., Holland, S. M., & Datillo, B. F. (2002). Crinoid distribution and feeding morphology through a depositional sequence: Kope and Fairview formations, Upper Ordovician, Cincinnati Arch region. *Journal of Paleontology*, **76**(4), 725–732.

Meyer, D. L., Vietch, M., Messing, C. G., & Stevenson, A. (2021). Crinoid Feeding Strategies: New Insights From Subsea Video And Time-Lapse. *Elements of Paleontology*. Cambridge University Press, Cambridge, UK.

Mitchell, J.S. & Makovicky, P.J. (2014). Low ecological disparity in Early Cretaceous birds. *Proceedings of the Royal Society B*, **281**(1787), 20140608.

Muscente, A. D., Prabhu, A., Zhong, H. et al. (2018). Quantifying ecological impacts of mass extinctions with network analysis of fossil communities. *Proceedings of the National Academy of Sciences*, **115**(20), 5217–5222.

Myers, C. E., Stigall, A. L., & Lieberman, B. S. (2015). PaleoENM: applying ecological niche modeling to the fossil record. *Paleobiology*, **41**(2), 226–244.

Nanglu, K., Caron, J. B., & Gaines, R. R. (2020). The Burgess Shale paleo-community with new insights from Marble Canyon, British Columbia. *Paleobiology*, **46**(1), 58–81.

Novack-Gottshall, P. M. (2007). Using a theoretical ecospace to quantify the ecological diversity of Paleozoic and modern marine biotas. *Paleobiology*, **33**(2), 273–294.

Novack-Gottshall, P. M. (2016a). General models of ecological diversification. I. Conceptual synthesis. *Paleobiology*, **42**(2), 185–208.

Novack-Gottshall, P. M. (2016b). General models of ecological diversification. II. Simulations and empirical applications. *Paleobiology*, **42**(2), 209–239.

Novack-Gottshall, P. M., Sultan, A., Smith, N. S., Purcell, J., Hanson, K. E., Lively, R., Ranjha, I., Collins, C., Parker, R., Sumrall, C. D., & Deline, B. (2022). Morphological volatility precedes ecological innovation in early echinoderms. *Nature Ecology & Evolution*, **6**, pp. 1–10.

Oksanen, J., Blanchet, F. G., Friendly M. et al. (2020). *vegan: Community Ecology Package. R package version* 2.5–7.

Pagel, M. (1999). The maximum likelihood approach to reconstructing ancestral character states of discrete characters on phylogenies. *Systematic Biology*, **48**(3), 612–622.

Paradis, E., Claude, J., & Strimmer, K. (2004). APE: analyses of phylogenetics and evolution in R language. *Bioinformatics*, **20**(2), 289–290.

Parsley, R. L., 1982a. Paracrinoids. In J. Sprinkle, ed., *Echinoderm Faunas from the Bromide Formation (Middle Ordovician) of Oklahoma*. The University of Kansas Paleontological Contributions, Lawrence, **1**, pp. 210–223.

Parsley, R. L., 1982b. Eumorphocystis. In J. Sprinkle, ed., *Echinoderm Faunas from the Bromide Formation (Middle Ordovician) of Oklahoma*. The

University of Kansas Paleontological Contributions, Lawrence, **1**, pp. 280–288.

Paton, T. R., & Brett, C. E. (2019). Revised stratigraphy of the middle Simcoe Group (Ordovician, upper Sandbian-Katian) in its type area: an integrated approach. *Canadian Journal of Earth Sciences*, **57**(1), 184–198.

Paton, T. R., Brett, C. E., & Kampouris, G. E. (2019). Genesis, modification, and preservation of complex Upper Ordovician hardgrounds: implications for sequence stratigraphy and the Great Ordovician Biodiversification Event. *Palaeogeography, Palaeoclimatology, Palaeoecology*, **526**, 53–71.

Perera, S. N., & Stigall, A. L. (2018). Identifying hierarchical spatial patterns within paleocommunities: an example from the Upper Pennsylvanian Ames Limestone of the Appalachian Basin. *Palaeogeography, Palaeoclimatology, Palaeoecology*, **506**, 1–11.

Peterman, D. J., Ritterbush, K. A., Ciampaglio, C. N. et al. (2021). Buoyancy control in ammonoid cephalopods refined by complex internal shell architecture. *Scientific Reports*, **11**(1), 8055.

Peters, S. E., & Ausich, W. I. (2008). A sampling-adjusted macroevolutionary history for Ordovician-Early Silurian crinoids. *Paleobiology*, **34**(1), 104–116.

Pianka, E. R., Vitt, L. J., Pelegrin, N., Fitzgerald, D. B., & Winemiller, K. O. (2017). Toward a periodic table of niches, or exploring the lizard niche hypervolume. *American Naturalist*, **190**(5), 601–616.

Pineda-Munoz, S., Evans, A. R., & Alroy, J. (2016). The relationship between diet and body mass in terrestrial mammals. *Paleobiology*, **42**(4), 659–669.

Polly, P. D., Fuentes-Gonzalez, J., Lawing, A. M., Bormet, A.K., & Dundas, R. G. (2017). Clade sorting has a greater effect than local adaptation on ecometric patterns in Carnivora. *Evolutionary Ecology Research*, **18**(1), 61–95.

Qian, H., & Jiang, L., 2014. Phylogenetic community ecology: integrating community ecology and evolutionary biology. *Journal of Plant Ecology*, **7**(2), 97–100

Rahman, I. A., Darroch, S. A., Racicot, R. A., & Laflamme, M. (2015). Suspension feeding in the enigmatic Ediacaran organism Tribrachidium demonstrates complexity of Neoproterozoic ecosystems. *Science Advances*, **1**(10), e1500800.

Rahman, I. A., O'Shea, J., Lautenschlager, S., & Zamora, S. (2020). Potential evolutionary trade-off between feeding and stability in Cambrian cinctan echinoderms. *Palaeontology*, **63**(5), 689–701.

Raia, P. (2010). Phylogenetic community assembly over time in Eurasian Plio-Pleistocene mammals. *Palaios*, **25**(5), 327–338.

R Core Team. (2021). *R: a language and environment for statistical computing.* R Foundation for Statistical Computing, Vienna, Austria. www.r-project.org.

Revell, L. J. (2012). phytools: an R package for phylogenetic comparative biology (and other things). *Methods in Ecology and Evolution*, **3**(2), 217–223.

Ricklefs, R. E., & Miles, D. B. (1994). Ecological and evolutionary inferences from morphology: an ecological perspective. In P. C. Wainwright and S. M. Reilly, eds., *Ecological Morphology: Integrative Organismal Biology.* University of Chicago Press, Chicago, pp. 13–41.

Robinson, D. F., & Foulds, L. R. (1981). Comparison of phylogenetic trees. *Mathematical Biosciences*, **53**(1–2), 131–147.

Sallan, L. C., Kammer, T. W., Ausich, W. I., & Cook, L. A. (2011). Persistent predator–prey dynamics revealed by mass extinction. *Proceedings of the National Academy of Sciences*, **108**(20), 8335–8338.

Schliep, K., Paradis, E., de Oliveira Martins, L. et al. (2021). *Package 'phangorn'. R package version* 2.7.0.

Schroeder, K., Lyons, S. K., & Smith, F. A. (2021). The influence of juvenile dinosaurs on community structure and diversity. *Science*, **371**(6532), 941–944.

Schumm, M., Edic, S. M., Collins, K. S. et al. (2019). Common latitudinal gradients in functional richness and functional evenness across marine and terrestrial systems. *Proceedings of the Royal Society B*, **286**(1908), 20190745.

Soul, L. C., & Wright, D. F. (2021). Phylogenetic Comparative Methods: A User's Guide for Paleontologists. *Elements of Paleontology.* Cambridge University Press, Cambridge, UK.

Sprinkle, J., ed. (1982a). *Echinoderm Faunas from the Bromide Formation (Middle Ordovician) of Oklahoma*, The University of Kansas Paleontological Contributions, Lawrence, Monograph 1.

Sprinkle, J., (1982b). Echinoderm Zones & Faunas. In J. Sprinkle, ed., *Echinoderm Faunas from the Bromide Formation (Middle Ordovician) of Oklahoma.* The University of Kansas Paleontological Contributions, Lawrence, **1**, pp. 46–56.

Sprinkle, J., (1982c). Astrocystites. In J. Sprinkle, ed., *Echinoderm Faunas from the Bromide Formation (Middle Ordovician) of Oklahoma.* The University of Kansas Paleontological Contributions, Lawrence, **1**, pp. 307–308.

Sprinkle, J., Theisen, L., & McKinzie, M. G. (2015). New camerate crinoid from the Late Ordovician (Sandbian) Bromide Formation, Arbuckle Mountains, southern Oklahoma. *Geological Society of America Abstracts with Programs*, **47**(7), 764.

Sprinkle, J., Guensburg, T. E., Rushlau, W. et al. (2018). New or more complete echinoderms discovered since 1982 from the Bromide Formation (Sandbian) of southern Oklahoma. *Geological Society of America Abstracts with Programs*, **50**(6), doi: https://doi.org/10.1130/abs/2018AM-319856.

Sproat, C. D., Jin, J., Zhan, R. B., & Rudkin, D. M. (2015). Morphological variability and paleoecology of the Late Ordovician Parastrophina from eastern Canada and the Tarim Basin, Northwest China. *Palaeoworld*, **24**(1–2), 160–175.

Stanley, S. M. (1970). Relation of shell form to life habits of the Bivalvia (Mollusca). *Geological Society of America Memoirs*, **125**, 1–282.

Stigall, A. L. (2012). Using ecological niche modelling to evaluate niche stability in deep time. *Journal of Biogeography*, **39**(4), 772–781.

Sumrall, C. D., & Gahn, F. J. (2006). Morphological and systematic reinterpretation of two enigmatic edrioasteroids (Echinodermata) from Canada. *Canadian Journal of Earth Sciences*, **43**(4), 497–507.

Sumrall, C. D., & Schumacher, G. A. (2002). Cheirocystis fultonensis, a new glyptocystitoid rhombiferan from the Upper Ordovician of the Cincinnati Arch – comments on cheirocrinid ontogeny. *Journal of Paleontology*, **76**(5), 843–851.

Taylor, P. D. (2016). Competition between encrusters on marine hard substrates and its fossil record. *Palaeontology*, **59**(4), 481–497.

Taylor, W. L., & Brett, C. E. (1996). Taphonomy and paleoecology of echinoderm Lagerstätten from the Silurian (Wenlockian) Rochester Shale. *Palaios*, **11**(2), 111–140.

Ubaghs, G. (1978). Camerata. In R. C. Moore and C. Teichert, eds., *Treatise on Invertebrate Paleontology, Part T Echinodermata 2*. Lawrence: Geological Society of America and University of Kansas Press, Boulder and Lawrence, pp. T409–T519.

Van Valkenburgh, B. (1994). Ecomorphological analysis of fossil vertebrates and their paleocommunities. In P. C. Wainwright and S. M. Reilly, eds., *Ecological Morphology: Integrative Organismal Biology*. University of Chicago Press, Chicago, pp. 140–166.

Vermeij, G. J. (1987). *Evolution and Escalation: an Ecological History of Life*. Princeton University Press, Princeton.

Villéger, S., Novack-Gottshall, P. M., & Mouillot, D. (2011). The multidimensionality of the niche reveals functional diversity changes in benthic marine biotas across geological time. *Ecology Letters*, **14**(6), 561–568.

Wagner, P. J., Kosnik, M. A., & Lidgard, S. (2006). Abundance distributions imply elevated complexity of post-Paleozoic marine ecosystems. *Science*, **314**(5803), 1289–1292.

Wainwright, P. C. (1991). Ecomorphology: experimental functional anatomy for ecological problems. *American Zoologist*, **31**(4), 680–693.

Walker, K. R. & Laporte, L. F. (1970). Congruent fossil communities from Ordovician and Devonian carbonates of New York. *Journal of Paleontology*, **44**(5), 928–944.

Walton, S. A., & Korn, D. (2018). An ecomorphospace for the Ammonoidea. *Paleobiology*, **44**(2), 273–289.

Webb, C. O., Ackerly, D. D., McPeek, M. A., & Donoghue, M. J. (2002). Phylogenies and community ecology. *Annual Review of Ecology and Systematics*, **33**(1), 475–505.

Webby, B. D., Paris, F., Droser, M. L., & Percival, I. G., eds. (2004). *The Great Ordovician Biodiversification Event*. Columbia University Press, New York .

Weiser, M. D., & Kaspari, M. (2006). Ecological morphospace of New World ants. *Ecological Entomology*, **31**(2), 131–142.

Whittle, R. J., Witts, J. D., Bowman, V. C. et al. (2019). Nature and timing of biotic recovery in Antarctic benthic marine ecosystems following the Cretaceous–Palaeogene mass extinction. *Palaeontology*, **62**(6), 919–934.

Winemiller, K. O. (1991). Ecomorphological diversification in lowland freshwater fish assemblages from five biotic regions. *Ecological Monographs*, **61**(4), 343–365.

Wright, D. F. (2017a). Phenotypic innovation and adaptive constraints in the evolutionary radiation of Palaeozoic crinoids. *Scientific Reports*, **7**(1), 13745.

Wright, D. F. (2017b). Bayesian estimation of fossil phylogenies and the evolution of early to middle Paleozoic crinoids (Echinodermata). *Journal of Paleontology*, **91**(4), 799–814.

Wright, D. F., & Toom, U. (2017). New crinoids from the Baltic region (Estonia): fossil tip-dating phylogenetics constrains the origin and Ordovician–Silurian diversification of the Flexibilia (Echinodermata). *Palaeontology*, **60**(6), 893–910.

Wright, D. F., Ausich, W. I., Cole, S. R., Rhenberg, E. C., & Peter, M. E. (2017). Phylogenetic taxonomy and classification of the Crinoidea (Echinodermata). *Journal of Paleontology*, **91**(4), 829–846.

Wright, D. F., Cole, S. R., & Ausich, W. I. (2019). Biodiversity, systematics, and new taxa of cladid crinoids from the Ordovician Brechin Lagerstätte. *Journal of Paleontology*, **94**(2), 334–357.

Zanno, L. E., & Mackovicky, P. J. (2011). Herbivorous ecomorphology and specialization patterns in theropod dinosaur evolution. *Proceedings of the National Academy of Science*, **108**(1), 232–237.

Acknowledgments

We thank J. Sprinkle for discussion of the age of the Bromide Formation and the diversity and status of Bromide crinoids and J. Koniecki for providing access to Brechin crinoid specimens. We thank B. Deline and J. Thompson for helpful reviews that improved this Element and thank C. Sumrall for organizing and editing this special volume. Funding for this research was provided in part by an Arthur James Boucot Award from the Paleontological Society (to SRC).

Cambridge Elements ☰

Elements of Paleontology

Editor-in-Chief
Colin D. Sumrall
University of Tennessee

About the Series

The Elements of Paleontology series is a publishing collaboration between the Paleontological Society and Cambridge University Press. The series covers the full spectrum of topics in paleontology and paleobiology, and related topics in the Earth and life sciences of interest to students and researchers of paleontology.

The Paleontological Society is an international nonprofit organization devoted exclusively to the science of paleontology: invertebrate and vertebrate paleontology, micropaleontology, and paleobotany. The Society's mission is to advance the study of the fossil record through scientific research, education, and advocacy. Its vision is to be a leading global advocate for understanding life's history and evolution. The Society has several membership categories, including regular, amateur/avocational, student, and retired. Members, representing some 40 countries, include professional paleontologists, academicians, science editors, Earth science teachers, museum specialists, undergraduate and graduate students, postdoctoral scholars, and amateur/avocational paleontologists.

Cambridge Elements ≡

Elements of Paleontology

Printed in the United States
by Baker & Taylor Publisher Services